VIBRANT VEGETABLES

JANNEKE PHILIPPI

VIBRANT
VEGETABLES

100+ DELICIOUS RECIPES USING 20+ COMMON VEGGIES

JANNEKE PHILIPPI

tra.publishing

Vibrant Vegetables: 100+ Delicious Recipes Using 20+ Common Veggies

AUTHOR, FOOD STYLING, AND STYLING

Janneke Philippi

CONCEPT

Studio Philippi

PHOTOGRAPHY AND DESIGN

Serge Philippi

EDITOR

Ingrid van Koppenhagen

U.S. EDITION PUBLISHER AND CREATIVE DIRECTOR

Ilona Oppenheim

U.S. EDITION COVER DESIGN

Jefferson Quintana

U.S. EDITION EDITORIAL DIRECTOR

Lisa McGuinness

U.S. EDITION EDITORIAL COORDINATOR

Jessica Faroy

Printed and bound in China by Shenzhen Reliance Printers.

Vibrant Vegetables: 100+ Delicious Recipes Using 20+ Common Veggies first published in the United States by Tra Publishing 2024. Text and recipes copyright © 2024 by Janneke Philippi. Photography and design copyright © 2024 by Serge Philippi. Original title: *Vega: 100 vegetarische recepten voor elke dag*. First published in 2022 by Nijgh Cuisine, Amsterdam.

ISBN: 978-0-9664388-7-1

Vibrant Vegetables: 100+ Delicious Recipes Using 20+ Common Veggies is printed on Forest Stewardship Council-certified paper from well-managed forests.

Tra Publishing is committed to sustainability in its materials and practices.

Tra Publishing
245 NE 37th Street
Miami, FL 33137
trapublishing.com

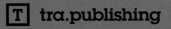

CONTENTS

Eggplant and Zucchini 10

Beets 42

Cabbage and Other Brassicas 64

Veggie Balls 90

Fresh Peas and Beans 110

Mushrooms 118

Legumes 134

Eggs 160

Leafy Green Vegetables 168

Tomatoes and Bell Peppers 180

Pumpkin, Squash, and Sweet Potatoes 200

Onions, Leeks, Fennel, and Asparagus 214

Winter Root Vegetables 240

Index 250

Vegetables are at the heart of my vegetarian meals. But scattered throughout the book you'll also find recipes that combine wonderfully well with the main dishes in this book. Homemade flatbread and smoked buffalo mozzarella are great appetizers to have with a drink. Crispy baby potatoes with lemon and crunchy artichokes with olive mayonnaise are perfect, festive sides. Meals for one or several meat-free days a week, for everyday eating, or for entertaining guests: I hope this book provides plenty of fresh inspiration for good food without meat or fish.

JANNEKE

Simply the best: these eggplants are baked whole in the oven. When done, they're topped with whipped goat cheese and seasoned with Tabasco, thyme, and poppy seeds. Delicious with bulgur wheat or pan-fried potatoes.

BAKED EGGPLANT
with whipped goat cheese and poppy seeds

SERVES 4

4 medium-size eggplants

2 tablespoons olive oil

6 ounces (200 grams) creamy goat cheese

2–3 sprigs of thyme

Tabasco

½ teaspoon poppy seeds

- baking sheet,

mixer (optional)

PREHEAT the oven to 400°F (200°C). Score the eggplants 3–4 times lengthwise. Place them on the baking sheet and drizzle them with the olive oil.

BAKE the eggplants in the preheated oven for 45–50 minutes until you can easily pierce the flesh with the tip of a sharp knife.

BEAT the goat cheese until creamy with a mixer or whisk. Strip the leaves from the thyme sprigs.

PLACE the eggplants on a plate, press down on both ends so that the score marks open slightly, and spoon the goat cheese crème into the slits. Drizzle on a little Tabasco, and sprinkle with the thyme leaves and poppy seeds.

Preparation time: 15 minutes
Baking time: 45 minutes

I start this dish by sautéing the eggplant slices to give them a bit of color. Then I braise the eggplant until its gentle flavor melds with the juicy tomato and the sweet soy sauce.

INDONESIAN-INSPIRED EGGPLANT
with tomato and sweet soy sauce

SERVES 4

3 ½ cups (700 grams)
white rice
2 medium-size eggplants
8 tablespoons sunflower oil
1 onion
1 tomato
1 teaspoon sambal
(Indonesian chili sauce)
3 tablespoons sweet
soy sauce

COOK the rice according to the package directions. Slice the eggplants into discs ¼ inch (½ cm) thick.

HEAT 3 tablespoons oil in each of 2 frying pans. Fry the eggplant slices until browned on both sides; they don't need to be cooked through at this point. Transfer them to a plate.

CHOP the onion finely. Dice the tomato. Heat 2 tablespoons oil in one of the frying pans. Sauté the onion with the tomato and sambal for 6 minutes, until it reduces to a thick paste.

STIR 6 ½ tablespoons (100 ml) water and the soy sauce into the onion-tomato mixture. Bring to a boil, then turn down the heat to low. Return the eggplant slices to the pan and cook for 6–8 minutes until done.

SEASON the eggplant with extra sambal or black pepper if desired and serve with the rice.

Preparation time: 30 minutes

As soon as I see croquettes on a menu, I'm sold. I love their crispy coating and surprise filling. The eggplant can easily be swapped out for zucchini. These croquettes are super simple to make, especially if you have some leftover rice.

THAI EGGPLANT-RICE CROQUETTES
with lime and cilantro

MAKES 8

1 medium-size eggplant

1 tablespoon oil

2 teaspoons Thai red curry paste

a handful of cilantro

½ cup (125 grams) cooked rice

4 tablespoons flour

zest and juice of 1 lime

1 egg

½ cup (50 grams) panko (Japanese breadcrumbs) or other dried breadcrumbs

oil for deep-frying

- plastic wrap

DICE the eggplant into small cubes no larger than ¼ inch (6–8 mm) (so that the croquette filling holds together well after shaping).

HEAT the oil in a frying pan. Fry the eggplant cubes for 8 minutes until browned and tender. Stir in the curry paste and fry 1 minute more. Transfer the eggplant mixture to a bowl.

CHOP the cilantro finely. Stir the rice and the cilantro into the eggplant. Add 2 tablespoons flour, the lime zest, and 2–3 tablespoons of the lime juice. Mix together (note: the mixture will be stiff). Season with salt and pepper.

SHAPE the rice mixture into 8 croquettes. Sprinkle the rest of the flour and the panko or breadcrumbs onto 2 different plates. Beat the egg in a deep plate. Roll the croquettes first in the flour, then in the egg, and finally in the panko. Place them on a plate covered with plastic wrap and refrigerate for at least 1 hour. This allows the croquettes to firm up and the bread-crumb layer to dry.

HEAT a generous layer of oil (about ½ inch or 2 cm) in a high-sided frying pan. Fry the croquettes for about 3 minutes until crisp and golden brown all over. Allow them to drain briefly on paper towels, then serve.

Preparation time: 30 minutes

Waiting time: 1 hour

Frying time: 10 minutes

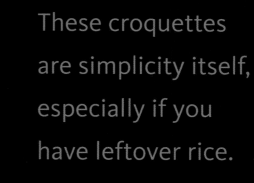

These croquettes
are simplicity itself,
especially if you
have leftover rice.

EGGPLANT SATAY
with ginger and peanut sauce

Peanut butter is simply ground
peanuts in a jar! Delicious with
sea salt, but also with sambal,
spices, or roasted coconut.

PEANUT BUTTER
with sea salt

Who doesn't love satay? In this recipe, marinated eggplant is threaded onto wooden skewers, grilled on the barbecue or in the oven, and served with a simple peanut sauce. Try swapping the sambal for Thai red curry paste and replacing the water with coconut milk. Serve with rice or noodles.

EGGPLANT SATAY
with ginger and peanut sauce

SERVES 4

2 medium-size eggplants

a 1 ¼ inches (3-cm) piece of fresh ginger

⅓ cup (80 ml) sweet soy sauce

2 garlic cloves

6 tablespoons peanut butter

1 teaspoon sambal (Indonesian chili sauce)

1 tablespoon dark brown sugar

2 tablespoons toasted, spiced coconut

- 12 satay skewers

CUT the eggplants into 1-inch (2-cm) pieces. Peel the ginger. Pour half of the soy sauce into a dish, then grate in the garlic and ginger.

MIX the eggplant into the soy sauce marinade and allow to marinate for at least 30 minutes. Meanwhile, if you're planning to grill the satay on the barbecue, soak the satay skewers in cold water to keep them from burning.

PREHEAT the oven to 450°F (220°C) or light the barbecue. You can also cook the satay in a little oil in a grill pan or frying pan. Thread the eggplant onto the satay skewers.

GRILL the eggplant satay in the preheated oven or on the hot barbecue for 8–10 minutes until cooked through and browned on all sides.

HEAT the remaining soy sauce in a saucepan along with the peanut butter, sambal, brown sugar, and ½ cup (125 ml) water. Stir until the peanut sauce is smooth.

PLACE the eggplant satay on a platter and sprinkle with the toasted, spiced coconut. Serve with the peanut sauce.

Preparation time: 30 minutes
Marinating time: 30 minutes

FRESH TOASTED, SPICED COCONUT Heat a little oil in pan. Fry 1 teaspoon ground cumin together with 1 teaspoon ground coriander. Stir in ¾ cup (50 grams) grated coconut and ½ cup (50 grams) shelled peanuts and fry until the coconut is light brown. Season with salt and allow to cool.

Ground up peanuts in a pot, that's all there is to peanut butter. For chunky peanut butter, stir in some finely chopped roasted peanuts. Or season it with sambal, toasted coconut, fried onion, or garlic.

PEANUT BUTTER
with sea salt

MAKES ONE JAR
2 ⅔ cup (350 grams)
unsalted peanuts
fine sea salt
- food processor or
immersion blender with
chopper attachment,
clean jar

ROAST the peanuts (in 2 batches) in a dry frying pan until brown. Turn them onto a plate and allow to cool.
PROCESS the peanuts in the food processor, or in batches in the chopper of the immersion blender, until very finely ground. Continue grinding until the oil is released and the peanut butter is creamy and nearly smooth.
SEASON the peanut butter with sea salt and spoon into a clean jar.

Preparation time: 15 minutes

Couscous with two of my favorites, eggplant and tomato, and mixed with some chickpeas, which are an excellent source of plant protein. Don't forget the lime wedges for a lovely note of freshness. Ras el hanout lends the couscous its beautifully aromatic flavor.

AROMATIC COUSCOUS
with eggplant, chickpeas, and tomato

SERVES 4

1 medium-size eggplant

1 ¼ pounds (600 grams) tomatoes

3 tablespoons olive oil

3 cups (300 grams) whole-wheat couscous

2 teaspoons ras el hanout (Moroccan spice mix)

9 ounces (250 grams) canned chickpeas

2 sprigs of mint

2 limes

CUT the eggplant into cubes and finely dice the tomatoes.

HEAT the olive oil in a frying pan. Fry the eggplant for 5 minutes until browned and cooked through. Stir the tomatoes into the eggplant and fry 5 minutes more.

PLACE the couscous into a dish and pour in 2 ¼ cup (500 ml) boiling water. Cover and allow the couscous to swell for 5 minutes.

STIR the ras el hanout and the chickpeas into the vegetables. Fluff the couscous with a fork. Stir the couscous into the vegetables and fry 1 minute more.

FINELY CHOP the mint leaves. Stir the mint into the couscous. Season with salt and pepper.

CUT the limes into wedges. Spoon the couscous onto a platter or 4 plates and serve with the lime wedges.

Preparation time: 30 minutes

Ras el hanout gives the couscous
a delicious spicy taste.

Eggplant can be found in practically every cuisine, including your favorite. It's one of only a few vegetables that are rarely eaten raw, but they're great in stews. This easy Greek stew is a real winner. Serve it with rice or french fries, a salad, and the roasted feta from page 125.

STIFATHO
with eggplant and Kalamata olives

SERVES 4

2 medium-size eggplants

2 onions

2 garlic cloves

4 tablespoons olive oil

½ teaspoon ground cinnamon

1 can (6 ounces/70 grams) tomato paste

¾ cup (100 ml) red wine

1 can (15 ounces/400 grams) peeled tomatoes

½ cup (100 grams) Kalamata olives

3–4 sprigs of oregano

CUT the eggplants into chunks 1-1 ½ inch (3–4 cm) wide. Finely chop the onions and mince the garlic.

HEAT 3 tablespoons olive oil in a Dutch oven or heavy-bottomed pan. Fry the eggplant until browned on all sides, then remove from the pan.

ADD the remaining tablespoon of olive oil to the pan. Sautéthe onion and garlic for 2 minutes. Add the cinnamon and the tomato paste and fry 1 minute more.

POUR the wine into the pan. Add the can of peeled tomatoes, ½ cup (125 ml) water, the olives, and the oregano. Bring to a boil, then turn down the heat to low.

RETURN the eggplant to the pan. Cover and allow to simmer over low heat for another 30 minutes, stirring occasionally. Season the stifatho with salt and pepper.

Preparation time: 25 minutes
Cooking time: 30 minutes

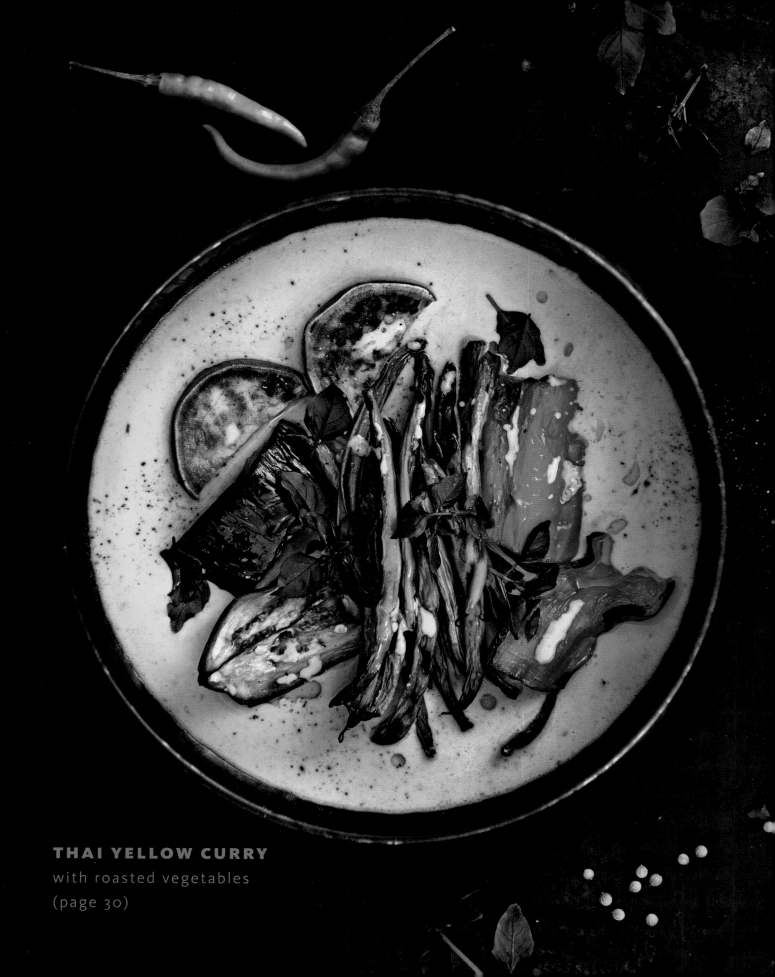

THAI YELLOW CURRY
with roasted vegetables
(page 30)

Thai curry pastes are made of a mixture of fresh chilies and various spices. The yellow paste derives its color from turmeric, which is also known as curcumin. Fresh chili peppers impart flavor and fire. You can add more or less, or a milder or spicier variety, depending on how hot you like it. It's the white membranes inside the chili that contain the capsaicin that produces the heat. For a milder curry paste, remove the membranes.

THAI YELLOW CURRY PASTE

PEEL and coarsely chop a 1-inch (2-cm) piece of fresh ginger. Also, coarsely chop 2 garlic cloves, 1 red chili pepper (or 1–2 green rawit pepper or bird's eye chili peppers) and 2 shallots.

PUT the ginger, red chili pepper, and shallot in the chopper and process until finely ground. Add 1 teaspoon coriander seeds, 1 teaspoon cumin seeds, ½ teaspoon ground cardamom, ½ teaspoon turmeric, a pinch of cinnamon, and a pinch of (freshly) ground nutmeg. Blend into a smooth paste. If necessary, add 1–2 tablespoons water to make a creamy curry paste.

SPOON the curry paste into a jar. Cover with a thin layer of oil, put on the lid, and keep in the refrigerator.

TOMATO

YOGURT AND DILL

BEET AND CUMIN

LIME, CILANTRO, AND GARLIC

It's surprisingly easy—and delicious—to make your own flatbread! You can prepare these flatbreads in advance and refrigerate them, wrapped in plastic wrap, for 1–2 days or freeze them for up to three months. Serve the bread at room temperature or reheat in a frying pan or grill pan over a low heat, until it's warm but not crisp. Great with the chickpeas with spinach in vadouvan sauce from page 157. I like to use vegetable juices, spices, and fresh herbs to add extra flavor and color to the flatbread dough.

FLATBREAD

BASIC RECIPE
2 ⅔ cups (350 grams) flour
2 ¼ teaspoons dried yeast
- food processor or mixer with dough hooks,
plastic wrap

KNEAD (with a food processor or mixer) the flour, 1 teaspoon salt, the yeast, and 1 cup (240 ml) water into a smooth, elastic dough. Sprinkle the salt into the bowl first and add the yeast at the end, sprinkling it into a well in the flour. This keeps them from touching each other, because salt inhibits the activity of the yeast.

ADD extra flour or water if the dough is either sticky or too dry. This might be especially necessary when using juice or a liquid with a slightly different consistency (see tips for varying the recipe on the next page).

SHAPE the dough into a ball and place it in the bowl. Cover the bowl with plastic wrap and allow to rise for 1 hour.

DIVIDE the dough into 8 equal pieces and roll them into balls. Heat a frying pan (don't add oil). On a lightly floured work surface, roll out a ball of dough into a circle about 1/3 inch (1 mm) thick. Place the dough circle in the hot frying pan and cook for 1 to 2 minutes, until the flatbread begins to puff up and turn light brown. Flip the flatbread and cook on the other side for 1 minute. Turn the heat down slightly if the flatbread gets too brown.

WHILE cooking the flatbread, roll out the next ball of dough so you can keep going. Keep the cooked flatbreads warm in a clean kitchen towel while you're cooking the other flatbreads.

Preparation time: 10 minutes
Rising time: 1 hour
Cooking time: 20 minutes

I like to give the dough for flatbread extra flavor and color with vegetable juice, fresh herbs and spices.

WITH BEET AND CUMIN

Replace the water with 1 cup (240 ml) beet juice and add 2 teaspoons ground cumin.

WITH TOMATO

Use slightly less water ½ cup (125 ml) and stir 1 can tomato paste (6 ounces/70 grams) into the water.

WITH YOGURT AND DILL

Replace the water with 1 ⅓ cups (350 ml) Greek yogurt and add a generous handful of finely chopped dill. For a beautiful green color, purée the dill with a few tablespoons of water. If the dough is sticky, add a little flour.

WITH LIME, CILANTRO, AND GARLIC

Add a finely chopped bunch of cilantro, the zest of 2 limes, and 2 grated garlic cloves.

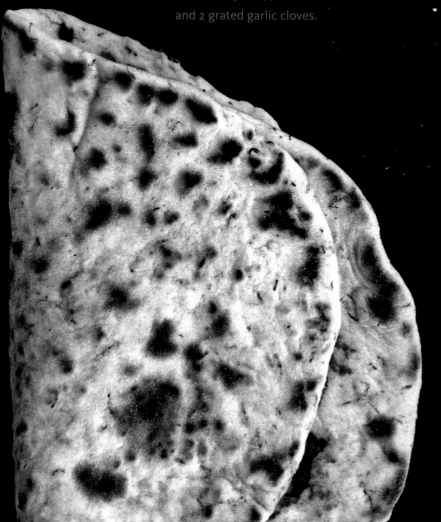

HARISSA COUSCOUS
with roasted vegetables

The sauce for this simple curry can be made while the vegetables are roasting in the oven. You can use a store-bought curry paste if you prefer— approximately 2 tablespoons—but homemade is tastier, of course. And you can make it as spicy as you like. Pressed for time? Make some in advance when you're not so busy. Curry paste keeps well in the refrigerator in a jar or other container, covered with a thin layer of oil.

THAI YELLOW CURRY
with roasted vegetables

SERVES 4

1 medium-size eggplant or large zucchini

2 bell peppers

⅓ pound (150 grams) green beans

⅔ pound (300 grams) sweet potatoes

3 tablespoons oil

1 ½ cups (300 grams) jasmine rice

2 tablespoons Thai yellow curry paste (from page 25 or from a jar)

1 can coconut milk (15 ounces/400 ml)

1 lemongrass stalk

a handful of (red) basil

- baking sheet with parchment paper

PREHEAT the oven to 450°F (220°C). Cut the eggplant or zucchini into 1 ¼-inch (3-cm) pieces. Slice the bell peppers into wide strips and remove the tips of the stem ends of the green beans. Peel or scrub the sweet potatoes and cut them into 1-inch (2-cm) pieces.

DISTRIBUTE the vegetables over the baking sheet. Drizzle them with 2 tablespoons oil and roast in the preheated oven for 20–25 minutes until done. Meanwhile, cook the rice according to the package directions.

HEAT 1 tablespoon oil in a frying pan. Fry the curry paste for 1 minute. Pour in the coconut milk. Bruise the lemongrass and add to the pan. Bring to a boil and cook for another 3–4 minutes until the sauce has reached the desired thickness.

DIVIDE the sauce and the vegetables over 4 plates and sprinkle with the basil leaves. Serve with the rice.

Preparation time: 20 minutes

Baking time: 20-25 minutes

An easy and delicious dish bursting with intense vegetable flavors. You can prepare the couscous and chop the parsley while the oven is doing its job. I recommend using a generous bunch of parsley or bulking it out with other herbs, including dill and cilantro.

HARISSA COUSCOUS
with roasted vegetables

SERVES 4

2 bell peppers

1 zucchini

2 red onions

4 tablespoons olive oil

1 ½ cups (300 grams) couscous

1 generous bunch of flat-leaf parsley

2–3 teaspoons harissa

- baking sheet with parchment paper

PREHEAT the oven to 450°F (220°C). Cut the bell peppers, zucchini, and onions into ¾-inch (2-cm) pieces. Distribute them over the baking sheet, and drizzle with 2 tablespoons olive oil.

ROAST the vegetables in the preheated oven for 20 minutes until they are done and nicely browned.

NEAR the end of the baking time, put the couscous into a dish and pour in 2 cups (500 ml) hot or boiling water. Cover and allow the couscous to swell for 5 minutes. Coarsely chop half of the parsley and finely chop the other half.

FLUFF the couscous with a fork. Stir in 2 tablespoons olive oil and harissa to taste. Stir in the vegetables and the parsley. Season with extra harissa or salt and pepper.

Preparation time: 15 minutes

Baking time: 20 minutes

I like to include a bowl of labneh in a selection of vegetarian appetizers. Goat milk yogurt needs to drain for at least a day or a night. If you don't have that much time, you could use Greek yogurt instead, which is thicker. Its mild and less distinctive flavor works just as well in this dish. These days, I tend to use two paper coffee filters instead of cheesecloth to drain the yogurt. Serve as a dip with flatbread, pita, and/or (roasted) vegetables.

GOAT LABNEH
with muhammara and dill

SERVES 4

4 ¼ cups (1 liter) full-fat goat milk yogurt or Greek yogurt

1 garlic clove

2 sprigs of dill

2 tablespoons muhammara (bell pepper spread)

3–4 tablespoons extra-virgin olive oil

1 teaspoon poppy seeds or finely chopped pistachios

- 2 coffee filters

PLACE a sieve over a large bowl. If using cone coffee filters, carefully tear open the filters on the perforated side and place them in the sieve. If using a basket filter, spread them out as far as possible. Make sure the filters overlap so that none of the yogurt can leak out through the sieve.

POUR the yogurt into the sieve, cover, and allow to drain for at least 10–12 hours in the refrigerator or a cool place.

GRATE the garlic and mix it into the drained yogurt (= labneh). Finely chop the dill.

SPOON the labneh onto a platter; spread it out with the back of a spoon, creating attractive grooves. Distribute the muhammara over the labneh.

DRIZZLE the labneh with the olive oil and sprinkle with the dill and the poppy seeds or pistachios.

Preparation time: 20 minutes
Waiting time: 10–12 hours

These easy-to-make eggplants check all the boxes: they're soft and spicy as well as crunchy on top. Serve with quinoa or (wild) rice and a bowl of olive mayonnaise (see page 210).

CRUNCHY EGGPLANT
with harissa oil and thyme

SERVES 2

2 medium-size eggplants

1 ½ tablespoons olive oil

2 teaspoons harissa

1 can peeled tomatoes
(15 ounces/400 grams)

2 garlic cloves

½ teaspoon ground cumin

2 slices white
sandwich bread

2 sprigs of thyme

- immersion blender with
chopper attachment,
baking dish

PREHEAT the oven to 400°F (200°C). Cut the eggplants in half lengthwise. Score eggplant halves crosswise; the score marks should be ½ inch (1 cm) deep. Mix 1 tablespoon olive oil with the harissa. Brush the cut surfaces of the eggplants with the harissa oil.

POUR the canned tomatoes into a tall measuring cup. Add 1 garlic clove, the cumin, and ½ (125 ml) water. Blend with the immersion blender into a smooth tomato sauce. Add salt and pepper to taste

POUR the tomato sauce into the baking dish. Place the eggplant halves in the tomato sauce, scoredside up. Bake in the preheated oven for 20 minutes.

PUT the bread into the chopper. Press in 1 garlic clove. Add ½ tablespoon olive oil along with the leaves from the thyme sprigs and process until finely ground. Add salt to taste.

TAKE the eggplants out of the oven and distribute the breadcrumbs over the cut surfaces. Return them to the oven and bake for another 20 minutes, until the breadcrumbs are golden brown and crunchy.

Preparation time: 30 minutes
Baking time: 40 minutes

This recipe can easily be scaled up to serve four, six, or eight people, making it an ideal dish for a dinner party or other festive gathering. Serve with white rice and a small plate of lime wedges on the side for a squeeze of freshness.

ROASTED ZUCCHINI
with chili soy sauce and sesame

SERVES 2

1 zucchini

2 teaspoons sesame oil

¼ cup (50 ml) sweet chili sauce

2 tablespoons soy sauce

2 tablespoons rice vinegar

a 1-inch (2-cm) piece of red chili pepper

1 teaspoon sesame seeds

- baking dish

PREHEAT the oven to 400°F (200°C). Cut the zucchini in half lengthwise. Brush the cut surfaces with 1 teaspoon sesame oil. Place the zucchini in the baking dish cut side down and drizzle the rounded tops with 1 teaspoon sesame oil as well.

ROAST the zucchini in the oven for 15–20 minutes until done. Meanwhile, heat the chili sauce in a saucepan along with the soy sauce and rice vinegar. Slice the red chili pepper into very thin rings and allow them to infuse the sauce.

TOAST the sesame seeds in a dry frying pan until golden brown, then turn them onto a plate.

TAKE the zucchini out of the oven. Pour the chili soy sauce over the halves, and sprinkle with the sesame seeds.

Preparation time: 15 minutes
Baking time: 15–20 minutes

At home, I like to put a selection of dishes on the table so everyone can mix and match to their heart's content. This recipe is great for such a buffet and combines well with the Hasselback beets from page 55 and the crispy lentil-truffle balls from page 107. An immersion blender makes quick work of the creamy hollandaise sauce with basil and Parmesan cheese.

SEARED ZUCCHINI
with Parmesan-basil hollandaise

SERVES 4

2 zucchini

¼ cup (25 grams) Parmesan cheese

7 tablespoonssalted butter

2 egg yolks

juice of ½ lemon

3 tablespoons olive oil

3 tablespoons (mini) basil

- immersion blender

SLICE the zucchini into spears. Finely grate the cheese.

MELT the butter in a saucepan. Put the egg yolks and the lemon juice into a tall measuring cup.

HEAT the olive oil in a large frying pan. When the oil is good and hot, place the zucchini spears in the pan. Fry them for 1–2 minutes on each side until they're golden brown and tender but still have some crunch.

MEANWHILE slowly pour the melted butter into the egg yolks and insert the wand of the immersion blender into the measuring cup. Blend until you have a thick, creamy hollandaise sauce. Add 2 tablespoons basil and the grated Parmesan cheese and blend until smooth. Season the sauce with pepper.

ARRANGE the zucchini in a serving dish and pour over the Parmesan-basil hollandaise. Sprinkle with the rest of the basil leaves.

Preparation time: 25 minutes

Just like mayonnaise,
Hollandaise sauce is
quick and easy
to whip with an
immersion blender.

This zucchini in crisp puff pastry is an easy entrée for two. All the prep can be done in advance. Cover the pastry parcel and keep it in the refrigerator until you're ready to bake it. Just brush with some beaten egg before sliding it into the oven. Serve with an extra grating of Parmesan cheese and a fresh salad.

STUFFED ZUCCHINI
with herbed ricotta in puff pastry

SERVES 2

1 zucchini

⅔ cup (150 grams) ricotta

a handful of grated Parmesan cheese

1 garlic clove

a handful of finely chopped herbs (chives, chervil, and basil)

1 lemon

2 all-butter puff pastry sheets, cut into squares

1 egg

- baking sheet with parchment paper, piping bag

PREHEAT the oven to 400°F (200°C). Carefully cut the zucchini in half lengthwise. Cut out the seeds with a knife. Use a spoon to scrape out a bit more of the flesh, hollowing out both halves down to the stem end to create an opening for filling the zucchini.

MIX the ricotta with the Parmesan in a bowl. Press or grate in the garlic. Scrub the lemon and grate the yellow zest into the bowl. Finely chop the herbs and stir them into the ricotta mixture along with salt and pepper to taste.

ROLL one square of puff pastry into a rectangle large enough to wrap around the zucchini. Press the zucchini halves together and wrap them in the puff pastry dough. Fold the dough closed on the rounded underside of the zucchini, but don't close the end with the opening for the filling.

SPOON the herbed ricotta mixture into a piping bag and pipe the filling into the opening at the top of the zucchini, then fold the end of the dough under to close, and place the wrapped zucchini on the baking sheet, seam side down.

BEAT the egg and brush it onto the dough. Bake the zucchini in the preheated oven for about 30 minutes, until cooked through and golden brown.

Preparation time: 20 minutes
Baking time: 30 minutes

Striking red in color,
this vegetable is sweet
and earthy in flavor.

SWEET-AND-SOUR BEETS
with rice vinegar and ginger

Striking red in color, this vegetable is sweet and earthy in flavor. These sweet-and-sour beets are a great side with spicy Asian dishes. Rice vinegar is sweeter and milder than natural or wine vinegar, but if you can't find it you can certainly use these other varieties. Feel free to add extra sugar or ginger syrup to taste.

SWEET-AND-SOUR BEETS
with rice vinegar and ginger

SERVES 4
1-inch (2-cm) piece of
fresh ginger
⅔ cup (150 ml) rice vinegar
2 tablespoons sugar
¾ pound (350 grams) red
beets
2 sprigs of mint

CUT the ginger into thin slices (no need to peel). Bring the rice vinegar to a boil along with the sugar and ginger. Allow the sugar to dissolve.

PEEL or scrub the beets. Shave the beets or slice them very thinly.

POUR the warm marinade over the beets. Tuck the mint in and among the beets and allow to cool. Cover the sweet-and-sour beets and keep them in the refrigerator.

Preparation time: 15 minutes + cooling time

Fresh noodles are so much better than dried ones, but not always readily available. The solution? Make your own! That way you can also make them as thick as you like. When served with some stir-fried vegetables and a simple sauce, the flavor of the noodles really comes into its own.

FRESH BEET NOODLES
with shiitake and sesame

SERVES 2

1 ½ cups (200 grams) flour + extra for dusting

1 tablespoon sesame oil

½ cup (100 ml) beet juice

1 teaspoon sesame seeds

1 lime

1 ½ cups (200 grams) shiitake mushrooms

2 tablespoons oil

3 tablespoons rice vinegar

5 tablespoons sweet chili sauce

- plastic wrap

PLACE the flour in a bowl along with ½ teaspoon salt, the sesame oil, and the beet juice, and mix together using 2 chopsticks. Continue kneading by hand until the dough is smooth. Add a little more water if the dough seems too dry, or a little more flour if the dough is sticky. Wrap the dough in plastic wrap and allow it to rest for 10 minutes.

KNEAD the dough on a floured work surface for another 10 minutes until it is smooth, elastic, and shiny. Wrap the dough tightly in plastic wrap again and allow it to rest in the refrigerator for 1 hour.

DIVIDE the dough into 2 pieces. Dust the work surface again with flour and roll each piece into a square that is ¾ inch (2 mm) thick.

LIGHTLY dust the dough with flour and fold it into thirds like a letter. With a sharp knife, slice the dough into ribbons of the desired width. Separate these ribbons and dust them with a little more flour. Repeat with the other piece of dough, slicing noodles of the same size.

TOAST the sesame seeds in a dry frying pan until golden brown, then turn them onto a plate. Scrub the lime, grate off the green zest, and slice the lime into wedges. Cut large shiitakes in half.

COOK the noodles in plenty of boiling, salted water for 3–4 minutes until done. Heat the oil in a wok and fry the shiitakes for 1 minute. Add the rice vinegar and the chili sauce and heat gently for 1 minute more.

DRAIN the noodles and stir them into the shiitakes. Sprinkle with the lime zest and the sesame seeds. Serve with the lime wedges.

Preparation time: 30 minutes

Waiting time: 1 hour

Cooking time: 15 minutes

FRESH BEET NOODLES
with shiitake and sesame

FRESH PLAIN NOODLES
basic recipe

PLACE 1 ⅓ cups (200 grams) flour into a bowl along with ½ teaspoon salt, 1 tablespoon sesame oil, and 100 ml water, and mix together using 2 chopsticks. Continue kneading by hand until the dough is smooth.

ADD a little more water if the dough seems too dry, or a little more flour if the dough is sticky. Wrap the dough in plastic wrap and allow it to rest for 10 minutes.

KNEAD the dough on a floured work surface for another 10 minutes until it is smooth, elastic, and shiny. Wrap the dough tightly in plastic wrap again and allow it to rest in the refrigerator for 1 hour.

DIVIDE the dough into 2 pieces. Dust the work surface again with flour and roll each piece into a square that is ⅛ inch (2 mm) thick.

LIGHTLY dust the dough with flour and fold it into thirds like a letter. With a sharp knife, slice the dough into ribbons of the desired width. Separate these ribbons and dust them with a little more flour. Repeat with the other piece of dough, slicing noodles of the same size.

COOK the noodles in plenty of boiling salted water for 3–4 minutes until done.

Mashed potatoes and beets with goat cheese and beer-soaked raisins—it's the Netherlands on a plate. These days, instead of wine, I like to add a splash of beer to my dishes. It gives a nice hint of bitterness. Port wine also works well with beets and goat cheese.

BEET AND POTATO MASH
with arugula and crispy goat cheese

SERVES 4

½ cup (100 ml) dark beer

1 tablespoon dark brown sugar

¼ teaspoon cinnamon

⅔ cups (100 grams) raisins

3 ⅓ pounds (1 ½ kilos) starchy potatoes

2 ¼ pounds (1 kilo) cooked red beets

4 tablespoons flour

8–10 tablespoons dried breadcrumbs

2 eggs

10 ounces (300 grams) aged hard goat cheese (flat piece)

3 tablespoons olive oil

3 ½ cups (75 grams) gently packed arugula

- potato masher

HEAT the beer in a saucepan along with the brown sugar and cinnamon. Remove the pan from the heat and add the raisins. Cover and allow the raisins to swell for at least 30 minutes.

PEEL the potatoes and cut them into 1-inch (2-cm) pieces. Add the potatoes to salted water and boil for ten minutes.

CUT the beets into 1-inch (2-cm) pieces while the potatoes are cooking, and then add the beets to the boiling water with the potatoes after they have been cooking for ten minutes. Continue cooking both the beets and potatoes for an additional ten minutes.

SPRINKLE the flour and the breadcrumbs onto 2 different plates. Beat the egg in a deep plate.

CUT the goat cheese into slices ¼ inch (7–8 mm) thick. Working with one slice at a time, press both sides into the flour, then dip in the egg, and finally roll them in the breadcrumbs. To make sure the breadcrumb coating is sealed, dip the slices in the egg and breadcrumbs again.

HEAT the olive oil in a frying pan. Fry the goat cheese slices for 5 minutes until golden brown and crispy on both sides.

MEANWHILE drain the potatoes and beets; save a cup of the cooking liquid. Mash them with a splash of the cooking liquid until creamy.

DRAIN the raisins. Stir the drained raisins and the arugula into the mash and season with salt and pepper.

SPOON onto 4 plates, and top with the goat cheese slices.

Preparation time: 40 minutes

BEET TARTARE
with soy sauce and sriracha

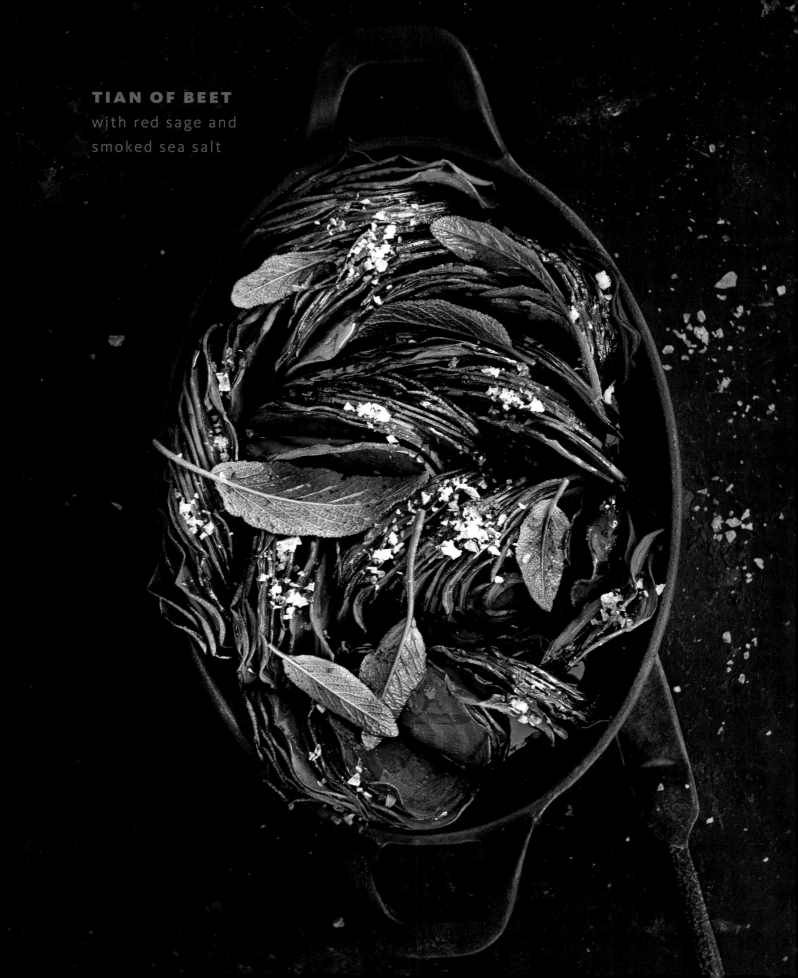

TIAN OF BEET
with red sage and
smoked sea salt

A vegetarian take on the ultimate French classic: steak tartare. We're adding a delicious Asian touch!

BEET TARTARE
with soy sauce and sriracha

SERVES 4

1+ pounds (500 grams) red beets

1 shallot

2 egg yolks

1 teaspoon mustard

2 tablespoons extra-virgin olive oil

1 tablespoon sesame oil

1 tablespoon soy sauce

2–3 teaspoons sriracha

1 teaspoon pink peppercorns

2 tablespoons shiso purple cress

WASH the beets. Cook them in plenty of water until done; this will take 40–50 minutes, depending on their size. Allow the beets to cool in the cooking water.

PEEL the beets, then dice them. Mince the shallot.

MAKE a dressing by whisking together the egg yolks, mustard, both kinds of oil, and the soy sauce. Stir the beets and shallot into the dressing. Season with sriracha sauce and also more soy sauce, if desired.

SPOON the beet cubes onto 4 plates (you can also use a plating ring for this). Crush the peppercorns between your fingers and sprinkle them onto the beets. Garnish with the cress.

Preparation time: 1 hour + cooling time
Finishing and plating: 15 minutes

A bit of olive oil, sage, and sea salt—that's all oven-roasted beets need. Sage comes in lots of different varieties. The red sage looks pretty in this dish, but of course you can use the more familiar green leaves.

TIAN OF BEET
with red sage and smoked sea salt

SERVES 4

1 ¼ pounds (600 grams) red beets

2 garlic cloves

6 tablespoons olive oil

(smoked) sea salt

1–2 sprigs of (red) sage

½ teaspoon ground cumin

- baking dish

PREHEAT the oven to 400°F (200°C). Peel or scrub the beets. Shave the beets or slice them very thinly.

STAND the beet slices on end in the baking dish so that they're touching. Slice the garlic very thinly, and tuck in between the beet slices. Drizzle the beets with 3 tablespoons olive oil and sprinkle with a little sea salt.

ROAST the beets in the preheated oven for about 45 minutes until done (you should be able to easily pierce the beets with the tip of a sharp knife.

REMOVE the sage leaves from the stems and marinate them in the remaining 3 tablespoons olive oil along with the cumin.

TAKE the tian out of the oven and distribute the marinated sage over the beets. Drizzle with the cumin oil.

Preparation time: 20 minutes
Baking time: 45 minutes

Large winter beets need more time than the smaller summer beets. They are done when a sharp knife slides easily through the beetroot.

Hasselback is a method of cutting slits into potatoes to create very thin slices that are still connected, which then fan out while roasting in the oven. It's a simple idea, which originated in Scandinavia. Sweet potatoes, butternut squash, and beets also lend themselves well to this preparation. The thinner the slices, the prettier the end result.

HASSELBACK BEETS
with thyme and feta

SERVES 4
1 ⅔ pounds (800 grams) red beets
1 bunch of thyme
3–4 tablespoons olive oil
2 teaspoons coarse sea salt
2 ½ ounces (100 grams) feta
extra-virgin olive oil
- baking sheet

PREHEAT the oven to 450°F (220°C). Scrub the beets and cut off the end with the leaves. Cut the beets into thin slices ¾-1 inch (2–3 mm) wide, to within ¼ inch (1 cm) of the bottom. In other words, don't slice all the way through the beets: keep the bottoms intact!

PLACE the beets on the baking sheet cut side up. Tuck the thyme sprigs into the slits. Drizzle the beets with the olive oil and sprinkle them with the sea salt.

ROAST the beets in the preheated oven for 45–60 minutes until done. The precise baking time depends on the size and kind of beet, and the larger winter beets need more time than the smaller summer beets. They are done when you can easily pierce the beets with a sharp knife.

TAKE the beets out of the oven and crumble on the feta. Drizzle the beets with a little olive oil and grind on more pepper.

Preparation time: 15 minutes
Baking time: 45-60 minutes

BEET DUMPLINGS

with green onions

MARINATED BEETS

with lime, coriander seeds, and yogurt

Making your own dumplings can be time-consuming, but they're worth every minute! These dough pockets are filled with a vegetarian ground meat alternative, beet, and green onion, but feel free to experiment; the combinations are endless. Add some chili flakes to extra soy sauce and serve this dipping sauce along with the dumplings.

BEET DUMPLINGS
with green onions

SERVES 4

1 red beet (180 grams)
1 cup (150 grams) flour
1 green onion
2 teaspoons toasted sesame oil
1 tablespoon soy sauce
⅓ pound (150 grams) fresh vegetarian ground meat alternative
- immersion blender, large biscuit cutter, plastic wrap, steamer, parchment paper

WASH the beet, then cook in plenty of water until done, about 45 minutes. Allow the beet to cool in the cooking water.

PEEL the beet. With the immersion blender, purée half of the beet along with ⅓ cup water. Reserve the rest of the beet.

PUT the flour into a bowl along with ½ teaspoon salt and the puréed beet. Mix together using 2 chopsticks. Continue kneading by hand until the dough is smooth and elastic. Wrap the dough in plastic wrap and allow it to rest for 1 hour.

FOR the filling, finely chop the reserved beet and the green onion. Mix the beet and green onion into the vegetarian ground meat-style product along with the sesame oil and the soy sauce.

DIVIDE the dough into 2 pieces. On a floured work surface, roll out one of the pieces of dough until it is ⅛ inch (1 mm) thick. Use the biscuit cutter to cut circles out of the dough.

SPOON a teaspoonful of the filling onto each dough circle. Moisten the edge of each circle with water, then gather the dough up over the filling to make little "purses." Place the dumplings on a plate covered with plastic wrap. Make the rest of the dumplings in the same way (about 30).

BRING a layer of water to a boil in a pan the same size as the steamer. Place the steamer on top of the pan. Place a piece of parchment paper into the steamer and add the dumplings in batches. Steam them until done, about 5 minutes.

Preparation time: 1 hour
Resting time: 1 hour
Shaping and steaming time: 15 minutes

Beets are delicious eaten raw. Uncooked, their beautiful red hue is probably at its most vibrant. Slice them very thinly and marinate them in a bright, citrusy dressing. The marinade softens the beets and imparts extra flavor.

MARINATED BEETS
with lime, coriander seeds, and yogurt

SERVES 4

2 small early red beets
(about 3 ounces/
80 grams each)
2 limes
4–5 tablespoons extra-
virgin olive oil
1 teaspoon coriander seeds
½ garlic clove
3 tablespoons Greek yogurt
a handful of watercress or
other microgreens

PEEL or scrub the beets. Shave the beets or slice them very thinly.

WHISK together the lime juice, the olive oil, and salt and pepper to make a marinade. Add the beets and stir. Cover and set aside for at least 1 hour to marinate, stirring occasionally.

MEANWHILE toast the coriander seeds until their wonderful fragrance is released. Coarsely grind the coriander seeds in a mortar. Grate or press the garlic into the yogurt.

SPREAD a circle of the garlicky yogurt onto each of 4 plates. Arrange the marinated beet slices on top of the yogurt in an attractive design. Drizzle with the marinade.

DISTRIBUTE the watercress around the marinated beets and sprinkle with the toasted coriander.

Preparation time: 20 minutes
Waiting time: 1 hour
Finishing and plating: 10 minutes

BEET GNOCCHI
with whipped ricotta and crispy sage

BEET AND QUINOA BURGER
with truffle sauce

To make these wonderful gnocchi, I replaced half of the potato in the basic recipe with red beet. You can also use other vegetables like squash, sweet potato, or cauliflower. Depending on the wetness of the vegetable purée, you may need to adjust the amount of flour for a firm, non-sticky dough.

BEET GNOCCHI
with whipped ricotta and crispy sage

SERVES 4

1 red beet (5 ounces/
200 grams)

1 large starchy potato
(7 ounces/200 grams)

1 egg yolk

1 ⅔ cups (250–275) grams
flour + extra for dusting

1 teaspoon fennel seeds

1 cup (250 grams) ricotta

extra-virgin olive oil

3 sprigs of sage

- food processor or
immersion blender, potato
ricer or grater, mortar and
pestle, mixer

SCRUB the beet and the potato. Cook them, unpeeled, in plenty of boiling water for 40–50 minutes until done. Take the potato out of the water halfway through the cooking time. Allow the beet and potato to cool at room temperature for 10 minutes and then peel.

CUT the beet into chunks and purée in the food processor or with the immersion blender. Mash the potato with a potato ricer or grater.

MIX the puréed beet and mashed potato with the egg yolk, flour, and a pinch of salt into a stiff dough. Add extra flour if the dough is too sticky.

ROLL the dough into ropes with a diameter of ½ inch (1 cm). Cut the gnocchi into 1 inch (2-cm) pieces. Press the gnocchi against a fork with your thumb to create a hollow on one side and ridges on the other. Place them in a single layer on a large platter that has been dusted with flour.

FINELY grind the fennel seeds in the mortar. Whip the ricotta with the mixer until light and creamy. Pour a generous amount of olive oil into a frying pan. Fry the sage leaves for 1–2 minutes until crisp but not brown!

COOK the gnocchi in plenty of boiling salted water for 3–4 minutes; they are done when they've been floating on the surface for about 1 minute.

REMOVE the gnocchi from the pan with a skimmer or slotted spoon and allow them to drain well. Divide the gnocchi over 4 warm plates and spoon on the ricotta. Drizzle with a bit of warm olive oil and sprinkle with the crispy sage leaves, the fennel seeds, and a little salt and pepper.

Preparation time: 30 minutes
Cooking time: 10 minutes

A vegetarian burger with beet, puffed quinoa, cumin, and garlic. Serve in a brioche bun with red lettuce and truffle sauce.

BEET AND QUINOA BURGER
with truffle sauce

SERVES 2

¼ cup (50 grams) puffed quinoa

5 ounces (200 grams) grated cooked red beets

3 tablespoons flour

1 teaspoon ground cumin

1 garlic clove

1 tablespoon mayonnaise

1 tablespoon crème fraiche or sour cream

1 tablespoon truffle tapenade

2 tablespoons olive oil

2 brioche buns

4 red lettuce leaves

2 tablespoons shiso purple cress (or other cress)

- immersion blender with chopper attachment

TOAST the quinoa in a dry frying pan until golden brown, then turn it onto a plate and allow to cool. Put the quinoa into the chopper along with the grated beet, flour, and cumin. Press in the garlic and process until everything is finely ground. Season the beet mixture well with salt and pepper.

MIX the mayonnaise with the crème fraiche and the truffle tapenade. Add more tapenade and pepper to taste.

SHAPE the beet mixture into 2 burgers. Heat the olive oil in a frying pan and fry the burgers for 5 minutes until cooked through and browned on both sides. Transfer the burgers to a plate and cover with a lid to keep them warm.

SLICE open the buns and place them in the pan, cut side down. Fry until the cut side is golden brown and crisp.

ARRANGE the lettuce on the bottom halves of the rolls, then add the burgers and a dollop of truffle sauce. Sprinkle with the cress and add the top halves of the buns.

Preparation time: 30 minutes

TIP Shape the beet mixture into burgers a day in advance, then cover and refrigerate. As well as being convenient, this also allows the burgers to firm up.

ROASTED CAULIFLOWER CURRY
with cilantro

CAULIFLOWER TEMPURA

with spicy mango sauce

Roasting really intensifies the flavor of cauliflower, which is perfect in a spicy Indian curry! Put the florets in the oven while you prepare the rice and sauce.

ROASTED CAULIFLOWER CURRY
with cilantro

SERVES 4

1 cauliflower

4 tablespoons sunflower oil

1 ½ cup (300 grams) basmati rice

1 red Romano (sweet pointed) pepper

2 tablespoons Indian mild curry paste

1 can tomato paste (2 ½ ounces/70 grams)

1 can coconut milk (15 ounces/400 ml)

a handful of cilantro

naan bread, to serve along with the curry

- baking sheet with parchment paper

PREHEAT the oven to 450°F (220°C). Divide the cauliflower into florets and place the florets on the baking sheet. Drizzle them with 2 tablespoons oil and roast them in the preheated oven for 20–25 minutes until golden brown and crisp-tender.

COOK the rice according to the package directions. Cut the pepper into strips.

HEAT 2 tablespoons oil in a frying pan. Fry the curry paste with the tomato paste for 1 minute. Stir in the strips of pepper. Pour in the coconut milk and bring to a boil while stirring.

ALLOW the curry to simmer for another 6 minutes over low heat. Now stir in the roasted cauliflower and season with salt and pepper.

COARSELY chop the cilantro. Spoon the rice onto 4 plates. Spoon on the curry and sprinkle with the cilantro. Serve with naan.

Preparation time: 25 minutes

Roasting time: 20-25 minutes

NAAN This Indian flatbread is often available in both plain and flavored versions. You'll find it on grocers' shelves alongside parbaked breads or with other Indian products. Naan tastes best served warm. Heat the naan in the oven or slice it into strips and toast.

Crispy battered cauliflower, served with a sweet and spicy mango sauce: what's not to like? Ice water is the secret behind the extra-crispy coating. Add two or three ice cubes to the cold water when making the batter. The fried florets are at their best straight out of the pan!

CAULIFLOWER TEMPURA
with spicy mango sauce

SERVES 4

1 small cauliflower
1 cup (150 grams) flour
3 ¼ tablespoons cornstarch
sunflower oil for deep-frying
½ cup (200 grams) mango chutney
2–3 teaspoons sriracha
½ lime
3 sprigs of flat-leaf parsley or cilantro
- paper towels

CLEAN the cauliflower and divide into florets.

PUT the flour, cornstarch, ½ teaspoon salt, and about 2 cups (240 ml) ice water into a bowl. Mix together with a fork into a batter the consistency of thick yogurt. Don't overmix the batter—small lumps are fine.

HEAT the sunflower oil to 350°F (180°C). Dip a small number of cauliflower florets into the batter and slip them into the hot oil one after the other. Deep-fry the cauliflower florets for about 3 minutes, until crisp and just tender.

REMOVE the cauliflower florets from the hot oil with a skimmer or slotted spoon and allow to drain on paper towels. Fry the rest of the cauliflower tempura in the same way.

MEANWHILE heat the mango chutney in a saucepan along with the sriracha. Add a squeeze of lime juice and keep the sauce warm over low heat. If the sauce gets too thick, add a couple of spoonfuls of water. Coarsely chop the parsley or cilantro.

ARRANGE the cauliflower tempura on a serving dish and pour over the mango sauce. Sprinkle with the parsley or cilantro.

Preparation time: 30 minutes

In the old days, cauliflower was often served whole. The popularity of stir-frying put an end to this, at least for a while. Now, though, it's back! Unusually for a quiche, this recipe features a whole one. It's an eye-catching centerpiece for the dinner table.

CAULIFLOWER QUICHE
with cheese and tarragon

SERVES 4

1 cauliflower

2 all-butter puff pastry sheets (frozen)

3 eggs

½ cup (125 grams) crème fraiche

2 sprigs of tarragon

3 ounces (100 grams) grated mature Gouda cheese

1 tablespoon olive oil

- greased springform pan 8 inch (20 cm)

CLEAN the cauliflower: remove all of the leaves and cut a slice off of the bottom. Cook the whole head of cauliflower in plenty of salted water for 8 minutes until just tender.

MEANWHILE preheat the oven to 400°F (200°C). Allow the puff pastry sheets to thaw.

BEAT the eggs with the crème fraiche. Finely chop the tarragon and mix into the egg mixture along with the cheese. Add salt and pepper to taste.

LINE the springform pan with the puff pastry, tucking any overhanging pastry back over the rim of the pan.

REMOVE the cauliflower from the water and allow it to drain very thoroughly. Pour the egg mixture into the puff pastry-lined pan, then add the cauliflower. Drizzle with the olive oil and sprinkle with a little salt and pepper.

BAKE the quiche in the preheated oven for about 30 minutes until done and golden brown.

Preparation time: 30 minutes

Baking time: 30 minutes

BEAUTIFUL WHITE Like white asparagus and Belgian endive, cauliflower effectively grows in the dark. White cauliflower has leaves that cover the vegetable as it grows and shields it from daylight to stop it from turning green. As well as white cauliflower, there are green, orange, and purple varieties too.

Teriyaki is a Japanese cooking method. "Teri" means luster and "yaki" means grilling or broiling. Teriyaki sauce is often used as a glaze for fish and meat dishes, but it's also surprisingly good with vegetables. Use a thick, good-quality teriyaki sauce or make your own. In this recipe, we roast red cabbage wedges with teriyaki in the oven and use one wedge to make a quick sweet-and-sour slaw as a refreshing contrast to the fairly sweet red cabbage teriyaki.

RED CABBAGE TERIYAKI
with star anise and sesame seeds

SERVES 4

1 red cabbage

6–8 tablespoons teriyaki sauce

½ cup (100 ml) rice vinegar

1 tablespoon sugar

2 star anise

1 teaspoon black sesame seeds

flat-leaf parsley or cilantro

- baking sheet with parchment paper

PREHEAT the oven to 450°F (220°C). Cut the red cabbage into wedges 4 cm wide. Reserve 1 of the cabbage wedges. Place the other wedges on the baking sheet and brush them well with the teriyaki sauce.

HEAT the rice vinegar along with the sugar and star anise. Allow the sugar to dissolve. Meanwhile, slice the reserved cabbage wedge into thin strips. Put them into a bowl and pour in the sweet-and-sour marinade. Give them a good stir and allow to marinate while the rest of the cabbage is in the oven.

ROAST the red cabbage wedges in the preheated oven for 20–25 minutes until tender and juicy. While the wedges are baking, brush them occasionally with the rest of the teriyaki sauce.

SPRINKLE the red cabbage teriyaki with the sesame seeds and the coarsely chopped parsley or cilantro. Serve with the sweet-and-sour red cabbage and noodles or fried rice.

Preparation time: 20 minutes
Baking time: 20-25 minutes

TERIYAKI SAUCE is easy to make by cooking equal parts soy sauce and mirin (rice wine) together with a splash of sake and dark brown sugar into a thick syrup. If you like, you can also add some lemon zest, grated fresh ginger, or garlic.

TRAY BAKE
with broccoli, baby potatoes,
and Vacherin Mont d'Or

Vacherin Mont d'Or is a seasonal cheese made of raw milk. It's only available in the fall and winter. The small round cheeses mature in a wooden box made from spruce, which imparts a unique flavor. For a quick and easy cheese fondue, slip the Vacherin into the oven for 30 minutes. Use the same tray to roast baby potatoes and vegetables for dipping into the divine, gooey cheese.

TRAY BAKE
with broccoli, baby potatoes, and Vacherin Mont d'Or

SERVES 2

1 pound (500 grams) broccoli

4 red onions

1 pound (500 grams) baby potatoes, unpeeled

3 tablespoons olive oil

1 Vacherin Mont d'Or cheese or Camembert in a wooden container (of about 16 ounces/500 grams)

2 garlic cloves

1 sprig of rosemary

3 tablespoons dry white wine

- baking sheet

PREHEAT the oven to 400°F (200°C). Divide the broccoli into florets and cut the stalks into 1-inch (2-cm) slices. Cut the red onions into wedges 1 to 1 ½-inch (2–3 cm) wide. Cut any large potatoes in half.

DISTRIBUTE the broccoli, red onion, and baby potatoes over the baking sheet and drizzle with the olive oil. Sprinkle with salt and pepper to taste.

REMOVE the plastic wrapper and the lid but leave the cheese in its wooden container. Cut several slits into the top of the cheese. Cut the garlic into slices and the rosemary sprig into pieces and tuck them into the cheese. Sprinkle the cheese with the wine and put the container in between the potatoes and vegetables.

BAKE in the middle of the preheated oven for 25 to 30 minutes, until the vegetables are golden brown and tender and the cheese has melted.

Preparation time: 15 minutes

Baking time: 30 minutes

OUT OF SEASON? When Mont d'Or is out of season, I replace it with a Camembert cheese in a wooden container.

Black kale, or cavolo nero, which is Italian for "black cabbage," is also known as palm tree kale in reference to its beautiful palm-like leaves. It can be prepared like ordinary kale and has an intense, earthy flavor. The chili in this recipe adds some heat. Alternatively, you can melt a piece of sharp blue cheese, like Gorgonzola or Roquefort, in the cream and finish the gnocchi with a sprinkling of chopped walnuts.

GNOCCHI
with cavolo nero, fennel seeds, and pecorino

SERVES 4

1 ⅓ pounds (600 grams) black kale

3 garlic cloves

2 tablespoons olive oil

⅓ cup (75 ml) dry white wine

7 cups (800 grams) (fresh) gnocchi

1 cup (200 ml) whipping cream

1 teaspoon fennel seeds

½ teaspoon chili flakes

pecorino, to serve

- mortar and pestle

REMOVE the hard ribs and slice the black kale crosswise into strips 3 cm wide. Mince 2 of the garlic cloves.

HEAT the olive oil in a high-sided frying pan and fry the minced garlic for 1 minute. Add the black kale and stir-fry for 2 minutes. Pour in the wine and cook the black kale for 8–10 minutes until done.

MEANWHILE cook the gnocchi in plenty of salted water until just done. Pour the whipping cream into a saucepan, and grate or press in the remaining garlic clove. Heat, and allow to reduce until the sauce starts to thicken. Grind the fennel seeds and chili flakes in the mortar until finely ground.

DRAIN the gnocchi and stir into the black kale. Pour over the garlic-infused cream and sprinkle with the ground fennel seeds and chili flakes. Serve with grated pecorino.

Preparation time: 30 minutes

GNOCCHI
with cavolo nero, fennel seeds,
and pecorino

Palm cabbage is another name for black cabbage. The name refers to the beautiful waving leaves.

Are you having guests over for dinner? This curry with wedges of pointed cabbage is sure to be a showstopper. The coconut milk adds a touch of sweetness and makes it all soft and creamy. Serve with naan bread or basmati rice.

POINTED CABBAGE CURRY
with sesame

SERVES 4

1 small pointed sweetheart or hispi cabbage (about 1 ½ pounds/800 grams)

3 tablespoons sunflower oil

1 onion

2 tablespoons Indian mild curry paste

1 can coconut milk (15 ounces/400 ml)

2 naan breads

1 tablespoon sesame seeds

8 sprigs of cilantro

REMOVE any unattractive outer leaves from the pointed cabbage. Cut the cabbage (lengthwise) into 4 or 6 wedges. Remove the hard core, but make sure that the wedges remain intact.

HEAT 2 tablespoons oil in a large sauté pan. Fry the cabbage wedges for 2–3 minutes per side until nicely browned. Meanwhile, finely chop the onion.

REMOVE the cabbage from the pan. Add 1 tablespoon oil to the pan and fry the onion for 1 minute. Stir in the curry paste and fry 1 minute more. Pour in the coconut milk and bring to a boil while stirring.

TURN down the heat to low. Return the cabbage to the pan. Cover the pan and simmer for 15 minutes until done. Turn the wedges regularly.

MEANWHILE heat the naan breads in the toaster (cut into wide strips) or grill pan. Toast the sesame seeds in a dry frying pan, then turn them onto a plate. Coarsely chop the cilantro.

SPOON the pointed cabbage curry into a serving dish. Sprinkle with the sesame seeds and cilantro. Serve with the naan.

Preparation time: 30 minutes

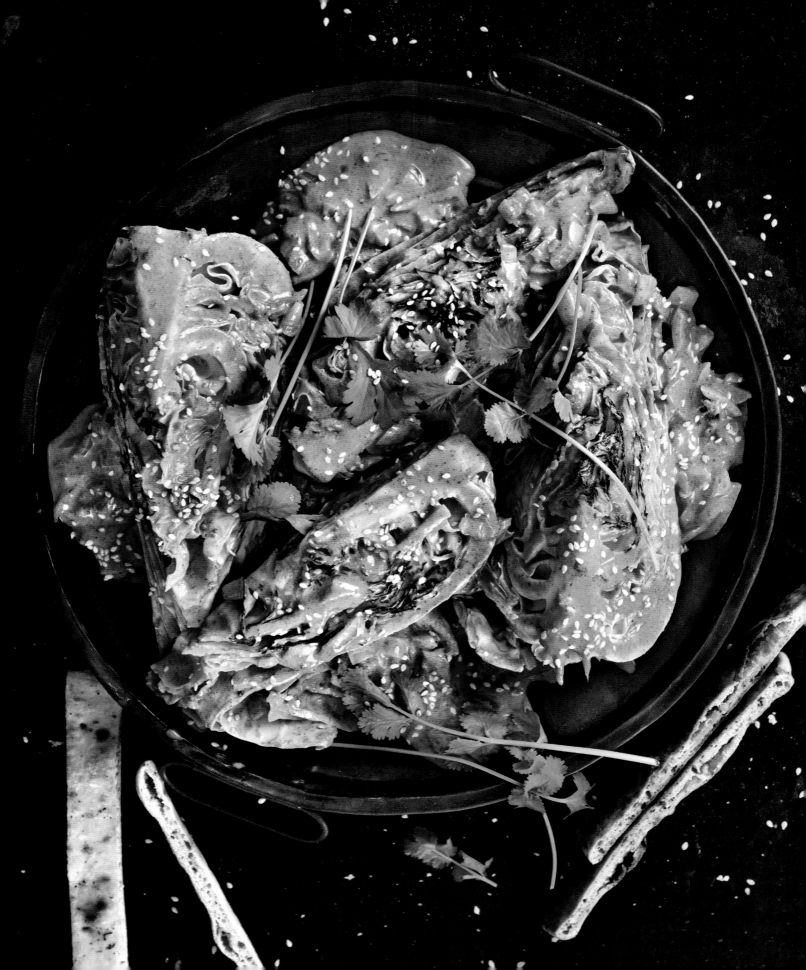

CHARRED BRUSSELS SPROUTS
with crème fraiche and pickled chili pepper

HASH BROWNS
with Brussels sprouts and mushrooms

When charring vegetables, the high heat darkens, almost blackens the outside in no time. This is often done on the barbecue, but you can also use the oven, griddle, or frying pan. After reducing the heat, the inside will soften and cook all the way through. The contrast between the intense, charred exterior and the mild, sweet center adds an extra dimension to the vegetables. If you want the smoky flavor without the charred bits, you can remove the blackened skin or outer layer.

CHARRED BRUSSELS SPROUTS
with crème fraiche and pickled chili pepper

SERVES 4

1 small red chili pepper

3 tablespoons rice vinegar

1 tablespoon sugar

1 ¼ pound (600 grams) Brussels sprouts

2 tablespoons olive oil

½ cup (125 grams) crème fraiche or sour cream

nutmeg

hash browns as an accompaniment (optional; see next recipe)

SLICE the red chili pepper into thin rings. Bring the rice vinegar to a boil along with the sugar. Stir until the sugar is dissolved. Pour the vinegar over the chili pepper rings and allow to cool.

CLEAN the Brussels sprouts. Heat a frying pan until it starts to smoke. Add the olive oil and then immediately add the sprouts. Fry the sprouts for about 4 minutes until they are charred all over. Stir frequently.

TURN down the heat and cover the pan with a lid. Braise the sprouts for 10–15 minutes until just tender.

DIVIDE the sprouts over 4 plates. Top with a dollop of crème fraiche, a sprinkle of nutmeg and garnish with the pickled chili pepper rings. Serve with hash browns, if you like.

Preparation time: 30 minutes

An American breakfast staple, I like to serve hash browns as a side dish with dinner. You can use this as a basic recipe to create your own variations. I've added Brussels sprouts and mushrooms here, but leek, spinach, parsnip, and squash are all excellent additions too.

HASH BROWNS
with Brussels sprouts and mushrooms

SERVES 4

3 ½ cups (500 grams) starchy potatoes

4 ounces (125 grams) Brussels sprouts

1 cup (125 grams) chestnut (cremini) mushrooms

1 green onion

2 heaping tablespoons flour

1 egg

6 tablespoons olive oil

- mandoline and plating ring 3-4 inches (8–10 cm) (optional)

SCRUB the potatoes. Peeling isn't necessary, but you can if you like. Coarsely grate the potatoes. Clean the Brussels sprouts and slice them into very thin strips on a mandoline or by hand. Clean the mushrooms with a brush and finely chop. Slice the green onion into thin rings.

PUT the grated potato into a bowl and mix in the sprouts, mushrooms, green onion, and flour. Beat the egg and mix into the potato mixture. Season the mixture with salt and pepper.

HEAT the olive oil in 2 or 3 large frying pans. If using a plating ring, place it in the pan. Spoon in a generous spoonful of the potato mixture, then press down on the mixture with the back of the spoon until it's about 1 cm thick. Fry for 1 minute, then remove the plating ring. Make 11 more hash brown patties in the same way. (If you aren't using a plating ring, add generous spoonfuls of the mixture to the pan and press them down with the spoon until the mixture is about 1 cm thick.)

FRY each hash brown patty for 4–5 minutes on each side until golden brown and cooked through.

Preparation time: 30 minutes

Young kale leaves are as tender as lettuce and can be mixed into the risotto raw. If you're using larger leaves, they can be chopped and braised in butter and white wine until tender. Truffle would be perfect with this dish, but the black crumbs that top this risotto are actually grated black garlic.

KALE RISOTTO
with black garlic and crispy kale

SERVES 4

2 shallots

2 tablespoons butter

1 ½ cups (300 grams) risotto rice

¾ cup (150 ml) dry white wine

4 ¼ cups (1 liter) vegetable stock

oil for deep-frying

1 cup (125 grams) young kale leaves

6 ounces (200 grams) Gorgonzola or Taleggio cheese

3 cloves black garlic

3 tablespoons extra-virgin olive oil

- paper towels

FINELY CHOP the shallots. Melt the butter in a heavy-bottomed pan. Fry the shallot for 1 minute. Stir in the risotto rice and fry gently until the grains of rice are translucent.

ADD the wine and allow the rice to gently cook until the wine has been absorbed. Now add the stock in 3–4 stages. Allow each quantity of stock to be absorbed into the rice before adding more. Stir frequently and cook the risotto for 18–20 minutes until tender but still firm.

MEANWHILE heat 1 ½–2 inch (3–4 cm) of oil in a small saucepan. Deep-fry ¼ cup kale leaves (in batches) for a few seconds until crisp. Remove the kale leaves from the oil with a skimmer or slotted spoon and allow to drain on paper towels.

DIVIDE the cheese into small pieces. Finely grate the black garlic and mix with the olive oil.

REMOVE the risotto from the heat. Stir in the cheese and the rest of the kale. Add pepper to taste, cover, and allow the risotto to rest for 3–4 minutes.

SPOON the risotto onto 4 plates. Drizzle the black garlic and olive oil over the risotto, and sprinkle with the crispy kale.

Preparation time: 30 minutes

Black garlic is fermented.
During fermentation,
the cloves turn black and
become silky and sweet.

When I plan to make fried rice, I try to cook the rice a day in advance. Chilled cooked rice better absorbs the aromatic flavor of the ground cumin and produces a fluffier dish. Quinoa is a tasty alternative to rice. This dish combines well with the eggs in soy sauce from page 162, or the eggs in peanut-chili sauce from page 165.

FRIED RICE WITH POINTED CABBAGE
and red-skinned peanuts

SERVES 4

1 ½ cups (300 grams) white rice

1 pointed (sweetheart or hispi) cabbage (about 1 pound/500 grams)

1 onion

2 garlic cloves

2 tablespoons sunflower oil

2 teaspoons ground cumin

3 tablespoons sweet soy sauce

⅔ cup (100 grams) salted red-skinned peanuts

Indonesian fried chili sauce

COOK the rice according to the package directions. Drain, and spread the rice onto a platter so that it cools quickly.

REMOVE any unattractive outer leaves from the pointed cabbage. Cut the pointed cabbage in half lengthwise, and cut out the hard core. Slice the cabbage into strips. Finely chop the onion and mince the garlic.

HEAT the oil in a wok. Fry the onion and garlic for 1 minute. Sprinkle in the ground cumin, then add the pointed cabbage. Stir-fry the cabbage for 6 minutes until done.

STIR the rice into the cabbage and fry for 1–2 minutes over high heat. Add the soy sauce and fry 1 minute more.

STIR in the red-skinned peanuts and season the fried rice with the pepper sauce and also a little more salt, if needed.

Preparation time: 30 minutes

On a cold winter's day, there's nothing better than a hearty sauerkraut casserole. A generous layer of sauerkraut covered with fluffy mashed potatoes and topped with cheese, baked in the oven. The combination of sauerkraut with red wine, apple, and thyme is one of my favorites.

SAUERKRAUT CASSEROLE
with red wine, apple, Brie, and thyme

SERVES 4

3 ⅓ pounds (1 ½ kilos) starchy potatoes

3 ½ cups (500 grams) sauerkraut

1 onion

2 garlic cloves

2 red Romano (sweet pointed) peppers

4–5 sprigs of thyme

3 tablespoons olive oil

1 can tomato paste (2 ½ ounces/70 grams)

¾ cup (150 ml) red wine

3 small honeycrisp or pink lady apples

⅔ cups (200 grams) crème fraiche

6 ounces (200 grams) Brie

- baking dish (18 x 28 cm)

PEEL the potatoes and cut them into pieces. Cook the potatoes in salted water for 20 minutes until done.

MEANWHILE preheat the oven to 400°F (200°C). Drain the sauerkraut. Finely chop the onion and mince the garlic. Dice the peppers. Strip the leaves from the thyme sprigs.

HEAT 2 tablespoons olive oil in a frying pan. Fry the onion along with the pepper and thyme for 2 minutes. Stir in the tomato paste and fry 1 minute more.

STIR in the sauerkraut and fry for 2 minutes. Pour in the wine and allow the sauerkraut to cook for 15 minutes.

SLICE off the tops of the apples and set aside. Peel, core, and dice the rest of the apple. Add the diced apple to the potatoes for the last 5 minutes of cooking.

DRAIN the potatoes and apple and mash them into a creamy purée. Stir in the crème fraiche and season with salt and pepper.

SPOON the sauerkraut into the baking dish. Distribute the mashed potato mixture over the sauerkraut and press the apple tops into the potatoes.

CUT the Brie into slices and place them on the potatoes. Drizzle with 1 tablespoon olive oil.

BAKE the sauerkraut casserole for 30 minutes until golden brown.

Preparation time: 30 minutes
Baking time: 30 minutes

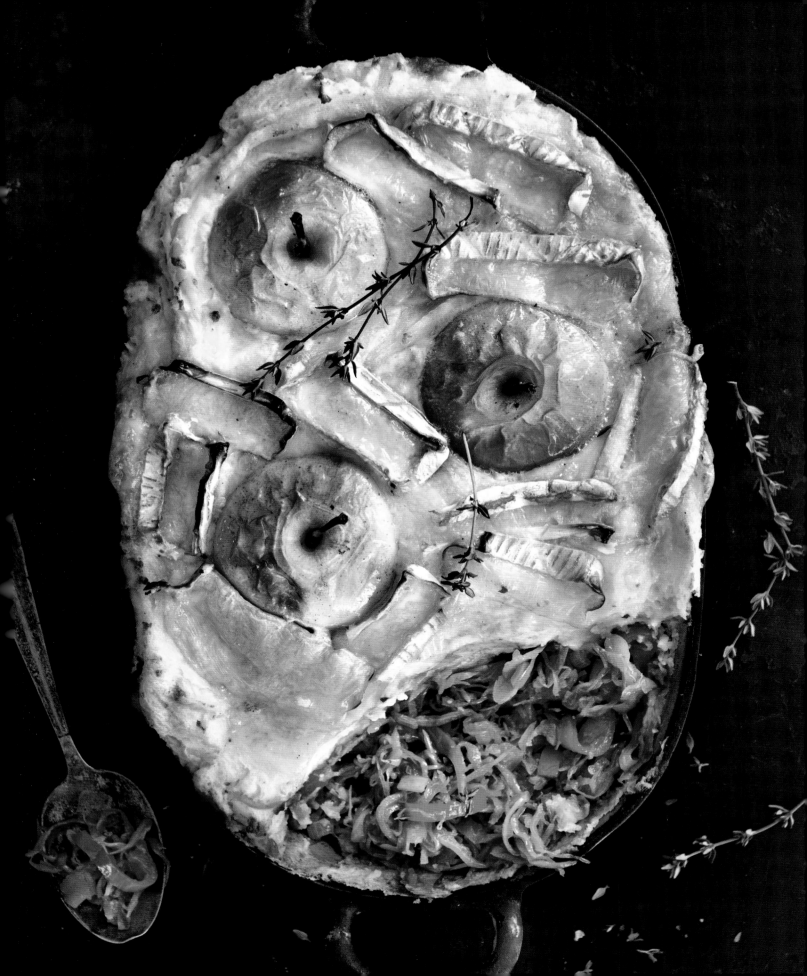

Take your time to shape the balls and, if possible, leave them to firm up in the refrigerator for a few hours. Once the prep is done, you'll have this dish on the table in a flash. Fried in a bit of olive oil, they're a great alternative to meatballs.

CHICKPEA AND TOMATO BALLS

SERVES 4–6

16 ounces (500 grams) canned chickpeas

2 ¼ cups (125 grams) semi-dried cherry tomatoes

½ cup (50 grams) dried breadcrumbs

- food processor or immersion blender with chopper attachment, plastic wrap

DRAIN the chickpeas well. In the food processor, process the chickpeas with the cherry tomatoes until finely ground (or do this in 2 batches in the chopper).

TRANSFER the chickpea mixture to a bowl. Mix in the dried breadcrumbs and season with salt and pepper.

WITH damp hands, shape the mixture into about 30 balls. Place them on a plate, cover with plastic wrap, and refrigerate for at least 2 hours to allow them to get very firm.

Preparation time: 40 minutes

Waiting time: 2 hours

For extra flavor, add finely chopped basil, dill, or tarragon.

While the chickpea and tomato balls from page 90 are resting in the refrigerator, you can get started on the rest of your meal. Great served with pasta and a salad.

CHICKPEA BALLS
in tomato sauce

SERVES 4

2 tablespoons olive oil

20–24 chickpea and tomato balls (from page 90)

1 14-ounce can peeled tomatoes (400 grams)

1 garlic clove

a handful of basil leaves

- immersion blender

HEAT the olive oil in a frying pan. Fry the chickpea balls for 6–8 minutes until hot and golden brown.

MEANWHILE put the tomatoes and garlic in a tall measuring cup and purée with the immersion blender.

TRANSFER the balls to a plate and cover with a lid to keep them warm. Pour the tomato sauce into the pan and heat for 4–5 minutes. Season with pepper and salt.

RETURN the chickpea balls to the pan with the tomato sauce and sprinkle with the basil leaves.

Preparation time: 20 minutes

You can easily give
tofu a flavor boost with
marinades or spices.

Tofu or bean curd is a kind of soy cheese. It's made by curdling soy milk (which is made from soybeans) with salt. On its own, it doesn't have much flavor, but you can give it an instant boost with a marinade. The drier the tofu, the crispier it becomes when you fry it. Pat the tofu dry or place it between two layers of absorbent paper towel an hour before use.

TOFU
marinated and crumbled

MARINATED TOFU For the marinade, stir together 2 tablespoons honey and 2 tablespoons soy sauce until well combined. Grate or press in 1 garlic clove and add ¼ teaspoon chili flakes. Cut 14 ounces (400 grams) tofu into slices ½ inch (1 cm) thick and pat them thoroughly dry. Place the tofu in a dish and pour over the marinade. Turn the slices over in the marinade and allow to stand for at least 15 minutes. Heat 2 tablespoons oil in a frying pan. Take the tofu out of the marinade. Fry the slices for 2 minutes on each side until browned, then pour over the remaining marinade and fry 1 minute more.

FRIED TOFU CRUMBLES Tofu can also be fried into crumbles and used in pastas, fried rice, or curries, to name a few. Pat the tofu thoroughly dry, then crumble coarsely with your fingers. With a spatula, fry the tofu crumbles in oil until browned. While frying, season the tofu with spices like ground cumin, coriander, and paprika, and lime or lemon zest or finely chopped fresh herbs.

The aromatic mixture of breadcrumbs, garlic, lemon, and rosemary adds a crispy coating to these roasted baby potatoes. They're bursting with flavor and delicious with the pumpkin confit from page 202 or the stewed onions with abbey beer from page 237.

CRISPY BABY POTATOES
with lemon and rosemary

SERVES 4

2 ¼ pounds (1 kilo) baby potatoes, unpeeled

3 tablespoons olive oil

2 slices white sandwich bread

1 sprig of rosemary

1 lemon

1 garlic clove

- baking sheet, food processor or immersion blender with chopper attachment

PREHEAT the oven to 450°F (220°C). Scrub the baby potatoes. Place them on the baking sheet in a single layer and drizzle on 2 tablespoons olive oil.

ROAST the potatoes for 20 minutes in the preheated oven. Meanwhile, put the bread slices (with crust) and the needles from the rosemary sprig into the food processor and process into fine breadcrumbs (or do this in 2 batches in the chopper).

SCRUB the lemon and grate the yellow zest into the breadcrumbs. Then grate or press in the garlic clove. Add 1 tablespoon olive oil along with salt to taste.

TAKE the potatoes out of the oven and crush them with the flat side of a large knife. Scatter the breadcrumbs over the potatoes.

RETURN the potatoes to the oven and bake for another 8–10 minutes, until the breadcrumbs are crisp and golden brown.

Preparation time: 20 minutes
Baking time: 30 minutes

I love eggplant and could eat it each and every day! With its mild, approachable flavor, eggplant works in virtually every cuisine. It's also one of the few vegetables that lends itself well to rolling into neat little balls.

EGGPLANT BALLS
in hoisin-ginger sauce

SERVES 4

2 eggplants

5 tablespoons sunflower oil

1 green onion

½–¾ cup (50–75 grams) dried breadcrumbs

2 ¾ tablespoons sesame seeds

1 garlic clove

a 1-inch (3-cm) piece of fresh ginger

4 tablespoons hoisin sauce

3 tablespoons soy sauce

3 tablespoons rice vinegar

2 sprigs of mint

- food processor or immersion blender with chopper attachment

CUT the eggplants lengthwise into slices ½ inch (1 cm) thick, then cut the slices into cubes.

VERHIT 1 tablespoon oil in a frying pan. Fry the eggplant cubes for 6–8 minutes until done. Turn them onto a plate and allow the eggplant to cool to room temperature. Finely chop the green part of the green onion.

PUT the eggplant into the food processor along with ½ cup (50 grams) dried breadcrumbs and the finely chopped green onion (or do this in 2 batches in the chopper). Process into a chunky mixture that holds together well. If necessary, add more breadcrumbs (up to ½ cup/50 grams. Season with salt and pepper.

ROLL the eggplant mixture into about 16 balls. Sprinkle the sesame seeds onto a plate and roll the eggplant balls in them.

MINCE the garlic. Peel and grate the ginger.

HEAT 3 tablespoons oil in a frying pan. Fry the eggplant balls for 5–6 minutes until golden brown all over.

HEAT the remaining tablespoon of oil in a saucepan. Fry the garlic and ginger for 1 minute. Add the hoisin sauce, soy sauce, and rice vinegar. Heat, and stir until the sauce is smooth.

TRANSFER the eggplant balls to a serving dish and pour over the sauce. Sprinkle with the leaves from the mint sprigs. Delicious served with rice and green beans or broccoli.

Preparation time: 30 minutes

Waiting time: 20 minutes

Polenta is made of yellow cornmeal and very popular in Italy. It's incredibly versatile and can be prepared in pretty much any shape or form, from porridge and pan-fried slices to fries and these little balls. With its mild, neutral flavor, polenta requires strong flavorings, and wild garlic provides just that. When it's not in season, you can also use a handful of arugula and one or two grated garlic cloves. Polenta bubbles and spits as it cooks, so I recommend using a large saucepan.

POLENTA BALLS WITH WILD GARLIC
in smoky tomato sauce

SERVES 4

½ cup (125 grams) polenta

a handful of wild garlic

2 ½ ounces (75 grams) Parmesan cheese

1 egg

2 garlic cloves

4 tablespoons olive oil

2 teaspoons smoked paprika

1 can tomato paste (2 ½ ounces/70 grams)

2 cans peeled tomatoes (14 ounces/400 grams each)

- plastic wrap, small ice cream scoop (optional), baking dish 8 x 11 inches (20 x 30 cm)

BRING 2 ½ cups (625 m)l water and 2 teaspoons salt to a boil in a pan. Sprinkle in the polenta and bring back to a boil while stirring with a wooden spoon. Cook the polenta over low heat for 8–10 minutes until done. Stir frequently and watch out for splatters!

FINELY chop the wild garlic. Grate the Parmesan cheese. Stir the wild garlic and the cheese into the polenta and add pepper to taste.

REMOVE the polenta from the heat and allow to cool for 5 minutes. Stir in the egg and allow to cool for another 20 minutes.

SHAPE (using damp hands) the polenta into about 24 balls (or use a small ice cream scoop). If you're using a scoop, dip it in water (as you would for ice cream) before scooping out the next ball. Place the balls on a platter covered with plastic wrap. Cover with plastic wrap and refrigerate for 8 hours to allow them to firm up.

PREHEAT the oven to 450°F (220°C). Mince the garlic. Heat 1 table-spoon olive oil in a frying pan. Fry the garlic with the paprika and tomato paste for 1 minute. Add the tomatoes. Crush the tomatoes with a spatula and heat the sauce for 5 minutes. Add salt and pepper.

POUR the tomato sauce into the baking dish. Add the polenta balls and drizzle them with the remaining 3 tablespoons olive oil.

BAKE the balls in the tomato sauce in the preheated oven for 20 minutes until golden brown.

Preparation time: 30 minutes

Waiting time: 8 hours

Baking time: 20 minutes

Small sushi rice balls filled with avocado, lime, and sesame. Do you miss the nori? In that case, you can finely chop a sheet of nori and mix it into the rice or serve each ball on a piece of nori. This recipe pairs beautifully with the sweet-and-sour beets from page 44.

SUSHI BALLS
with marinated avocado

SERVES 4

1 ¼ cups (250 grams) sushi rice

a 3-cm piece of fresh ginger

1 star anise

¼ cup (75 ml) soy sauce

5 tablespoons rice vinegar

1 teaspoon sugar

1 teaspoon wasabi paste

1 tablespoon mayonnaise

1 lime

1 teaspoon sesame oil

½ avocado

shiso purple cress, water-cress or other microgreens

2 teaspoons black sesame seeds

- small piping bag (optional)

BRING the sushi rice and 2 cups (350 ml) water to a boil. Turn down the heat to low, cover, and allow the rice to cook gently for 10 minutes. Remove the pan from the heat. Allow the rice to stand for another 15 minutes (covered). Allow the rice to cool to room temperature.

PEEL the ginger and cut into long strips with a vegetable peeler. Put the ginger and the star anise into a small bowl and pour in the soy sauce. Set this sauce aside.

HEAT the rice vinegar along with the sugar and 1 teaspoon salt until the sugar has dissolved. Allow the sweet-and-sour marinade to cool to room temperature, then stir into the rice.

STIR the wasabi and mayonnaise until well combined. For a milder flavor, add more mayonnaise.

SCRUB the lime and grate off the green zest. Squeeze half of the lime. In a small bowl, mix the lime juice and zest with the sesame oil.

CUT the avocado in half and remove the pit and peel. Cut the avocado into cubes no larger than 1 cm, then stir them into the lime-sesame marinade.

SHAPE the rice into about 20 balls (using damp hands—make sure they're not too wet!). Press a cube of marinated avocado into every ball, then roll it closed again. Place the balls on a platter.

GARNISH each sushi ball with a dab of wasabi mayonnaise (you can use a small piping bag for this if you like). Sprinkle with the shiso purple cress and the sesame seeds. Serve with the soy-ginger sauce.

Preparation time: 30 minutes + cooling time
Finishing and assembly: 30 minutes

HEARTY HERB AND LEMON BALLS
with Parmesan

CRISPY LENTIL-TRUFFLE BALLS
with truffle-Parmesan mayonnaise

Vegetarian and vegan ground meat alternatives are widely available these days, usually made with soy protein. You can cook them as they are or shape them into burgers, patties, or balls. Here they're flavored with fresh herbs, lemon, chili, and Parmesan cheese. Ginger and spices are great seasonings, too. Eat them in a traditional dish of pasta and tomato sauce, or with pan-fried potatoes and a salad.

HEARTY HERB AND LEMON BALLS
with Parmesan

SERVES 4

15 ounces (400 grams) fresh vegetarian ground meat alternative

2 lemons

2 garlic cloves

a handful of fresh herbs (such as parsley, chives, and basil)

a handful of grated Parmesan cheese

¼ teaspoon chili flakes

3 tablespoons olive oil

PLACE the vegetarian ground meat alternative in a bowl. Scrub the lemons, then grate the yellow zest and also the garlic into the bowl.

FINELY CHOP the herbs, add them to the bowl, and mix them in along with the Parmesan, chili flakes, and a little salt and pepper. Shape the mixture into smaller or larger balls, depending on how you like them.

HEAT the olive oil in a frying pan. Fry the herb and lemon balls for 10 minutes until browned and cooked through. Once they're out of the pan, go ahead and sprinkle on more herbs, lemon zest, and chili flakes.

Preparation time: 30 minutes

Lentils and mushrooms are the perfect base for these crispy balls. The addition of truffle makes them perfect for a festive occasion! Great with french fries with Parmesan cheese and an arugula salad.

CRISPY LENTIL-TRUFFLE BALLS
with truffle-Parmesan mayonnaise

SERVES 4

1 ½ cups (200 grams) chestnut (cremini) mushrooms

1 sprig of rosemary

2 garlic cloves

olive oil for frying

3 tablespoons truffle tapenade

12 ounces (300 grams) canned lentils

3 tablespoons flour

¼ cup (25 grams) panko (Japanese breadcrumbs)

2 tablespoons grated Parmesan cheese

2 tablespoons mayonnaise

- food processor or immersion blender with chopper attachment, paper towels

PROCESS the mushrooms and the needles from the rosemary sprig in the food processor or chopper until finely ground. Press or grate in the garlic.

HEAT 1 tablespoon olive oil in a frying pan. Fry the mushroom mixture for 4–5 minutes until all of the liquid has evaporated. Stir in 1 tablespoon truffle tapenade.

MEANWHILE drain the lentils thoroughly. Coarsely chop them in the food processor or chopper. Transfer the lentils to a bowl and stir in the mushroom mixture and the flour. Season with salt and pepper.

WITH damp hands, shape the lentil-mushroom mixture into about 20 small balls. Sprinkle the panko onto a plate and roll the balls in the breadcrumbs.

HEAT a generous layer of olive oil in a frying pan. Fry the lentil balls for 4–5 minutes until crisp and golden brown. Meanwhile, mix the remaining 2 tablespoons truffle tapenade, the Parmesan cheese, and pepper to taste into the mayonnaise.

TAKE the balls out of the oil with a skimmer or slotted spoon and allow to drain on paper towels. Serve the crispy lentil-truffle balls with the truffle-Parmesan mayonnaise.

Preparation time: 30 minutes
Frying time: 15 minutes

They're delicious, these little balls made from ricotta, flour, and Parmesan. Ricotta is often flavored with fresh herbs and lemon and pairs well with a simple tomato sauce. But here we're going for luxury with saffron cream. Lemon balm intensifies the lemony aroma, but basil or arugula are equally good garnishes. The roasted green beans with chili and caper salsa from page 112 are a spicy foil to the creamy little balls.

LEMON-RICOTTA BALLS
with saffron cream

SERVES 2

⅔ cup (75 ml) dry white wine

1 small pinch of saffron (0.05 grams)

1 cup (250 grams) ricotta

1 egg yolk

2 ½ ounces (25 grams) grated Parmesan cheese

½ cup (75 grams) flour

a handful of basil or arugula

1 lemon

1 shallot

1 cup (200 ml) whipping cream

1 sprig of lemon balm

- plastic wrap

POUR the wine into a saucepan, sprinkle in the saffron, and allow to soak.

PLACE the ricotta into a bowl and mix in the egg yolk, Parmesan, flour, and a pinch of salt. Finely chop the basil or arugula and stir into the ricotta mixture.

SCRUB the lemon and grate the yellow zest into the bowl. Add salt and pepper to taste and stir until well mixed.

SHAPE (using damp hands) the ricotta mixture into 16 balls. Place them on a plate covered with plastic wrap.

MINCE the shallot and stir it into the saffron soaking liquid. Bring to a boil and allow the wine to reduce to 2–3 tablespoons. Add the whipping cream and cook for 4–5 minutes until it has reduced to a sauce.

SLIP the ricotta balls gently into a large pan of boiling salted water. Cook them for 4–5 minutes—the balls will rise to the surface when done. Remove them from the pan with a skimmer or slotted spoon. Allow them to drain briefly, then put them into the saffron cream. Season with salt and pepper.

DIVIDE the ricotta balls and saffron cream over 2 plates, and garnish with the lemon balm.

Preparation time: 40 minutes

I make some type of curry most weeks, as they offer endless variation. Sometimes I'll add a handful of cherry tomatoes to this recipe, or I'll swap the tofu for paneer, an Indian fresh cheese made from cow's milk. Paneer is an animal product, while tofu is plant-based. Both are rich in protein.

GREEN CURRY
with sugar snap peas, tofu, and sticky peanuts

SERVES 4

1 ½ cups (300 grams) basmati rice

14 ounces (400 grams) tofu

2 green bell peppers

2 tablespoons oil

2 tablespoons Indian mild curry paste

2 pounds (400 grams) sugar snap peas

1 can coconut milk (15 ounces/400 ml)

½ cup (75 grams) unsalted peanuts

1 tablespoon ginger syrup

2 green onions

- parchment paper

COOK the rice according to the package directions. Cut the tofu into cubes and pat them with paper towels until thoroughly dry. Chop the bell peppers.

HEAT the oil in a frying pan. Fry the tofu for 3 minutes until browned, then remove from the pan. Add more oil if necessary and stir-fry the bell pepper and sugar snap peas for 3 minutes. Stir in the curry paste and fry 1 minute more.

RETURN the tofu to the pan and pour in the coconut milk. Bring just to a boil and allow the curry to simmer for another 10 minutes, until the sauce has reduced to the desired thickness.

TOAST the peanuts in a dry frying pan until they're golden brown. Pour in the ginger syrup and fry for another 1–2 minutes until the syrup sticks to the peanuts and has caramelized.

TIP the peanuts onto a plate covered with a sheet of parchment paper and allow to cool. Separate the peanuts where you can. Slice the green onions into rings.

SPOON the curry into 4 deep plates. Sprinkle with the peanuts and green onions. Serve with the rice.

Preparation time: 30 minutes

Roasting the green beans in a little oil gives them a more intense, almost nutty flavor. If you like, you can prepare them in advance and leave them to cool to room temperature. Spoon over the salty, punchy salsa of fried capers, red bell pepper, and pine nuts just before serving.

HARICOTS VERTS (THIN GREEN BEANS)
with chili and caper salsa

SERVES 4

1 ¼ pounds (500 grams) haricots verts (or thin green beans)

3 tablespoons olive oil

1 red chili pepper

2 tablespoons capers

1 tablespoon pine nuts

extra-virgin olive oil

PUT a large frying pan on the stove to preheat. Meanwhile, cut the tips of the stem ends off of the haricots verts or thin green beans and toss them in 2 tablespoons olive oil.

SAUTÉ the haricots verts or green beans for 4–5 minutes until brown (almost black) and just tender.

CUT the red chili pepper in half, remove the seeds and membrane, and finely chop. Coarsely chop the capers.

PLACE the haricots verts into a serving dish. If you want to serve the beans warm, cover with a lid or aluminum foil.

POUR 1 tablespoon olive oil into the frying pan. Fry the pine nuts until golden brown. Add the red chili pepper and the capers and fry for 1 minute more. Sprinkle with a little salt.

SPOON the chili and caper salsa over the haricots verts, and finish with a splash of extra-virgin olive oil.

Preparation time: 20 minutes

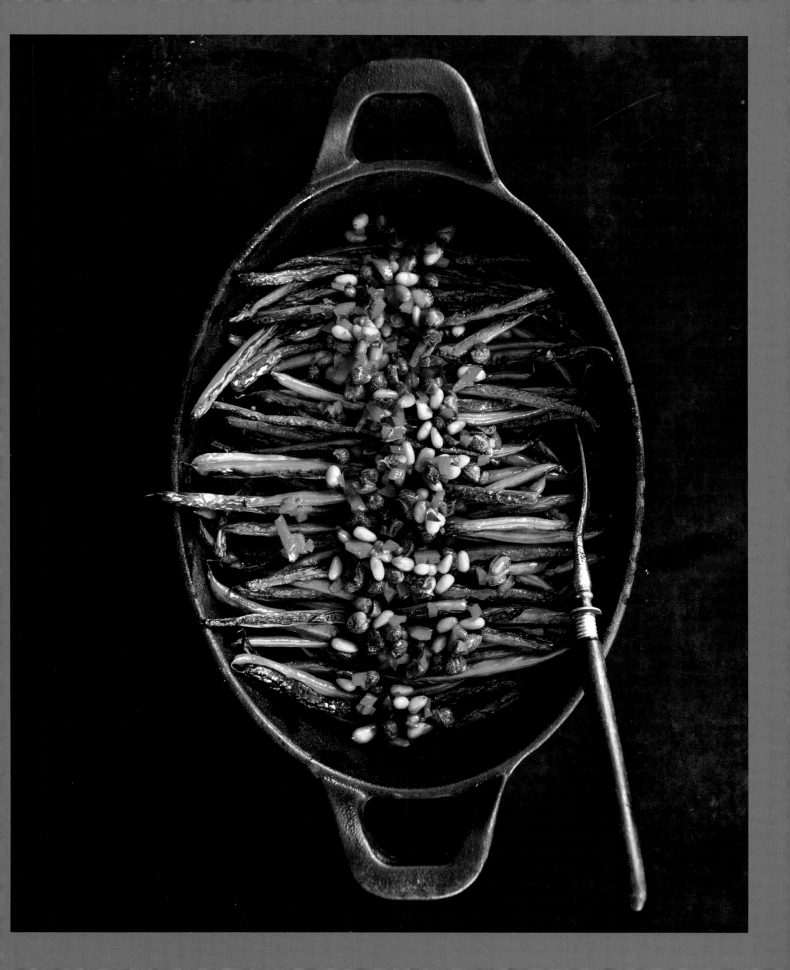

This sushi roll not only looks exquisite, its filling of marinated soybeans with avocado, sesame oil, and chili-lime mayonnaise tastes delicious too. Serve with extra chili-lime mayonnaise and a bowl of soy sauce for dipping.

SUSHI ROLL WITH EDAMAME
and green chili-lime mayonnaise

SERVES 2

1 cup (200 grams) sushi rice

zest and juice of 2 limes

1 egg

1 teaspoon mustard

1 cup (225 ml) sunflower oil

1–2 tablespoons Thai green sweet chili sauce

4 tablespoons rice vinegar

1 teaspoon sugar

a ½-inch (1-cm) piece of fresh ginger

1 teaspoon sesame oil

1 avocado

½ cup (50 grams) edamame

2 sheets of nori

2 teaspoons black sesame seeds

cress to garnish

3 tablespoons soy sauce

- immersion blender, bamboo sushi mat, plastic wrap

MAKE the sushi rice according to the package directions. Allow the rice to cool to room temperature.

PLACE half of the lime juice into a tall measuring cup along with the egg, mustard, and sunflower oil. Insert the wand of the immersion blender and blend into a thick, creamy mayonnaise. Season with the lime zest and green chili sauce.

HEAT the rice vinegar with the sugar and 1 teaspoon salt. Allow this sweet-and-sour marinade to cool, then stir into the rice.

PEEL and grate the ginger. Mix the ginger with the rest of the lime juice and the sesame oil.

CUT the avocado into strips. Mix the avocado and half of the soybeans into the ginger-lime-sesame marinade.

PLACE a piece of plastic wrap onto the sushi mat and top with a sheet of nori, smooth side down. With damp hands, distribute half of the rice over the nori, staying back 1 inch (2 cm) from the top edge.

ARRANGE half of the marinated avocado and soybeans over the bottom quarter of the sheet of nori. Pipe or spoon on a line of chili-lime mayonnaise alongside this.

ROLL up the nori with the sushi rice and filling. Place the sushi roll onto a platter, seam side down, and make one more roll. Neatly trim the ends of the rolls.

PLACE the sushi rolls on 2 plates. Distribute the rest of the soybeans over the rolls. Sprinkle with the sesame seeds and a little cress. Serve the sushi rolls with soy sauce and more chili-lime mayonnaise.

Preparation time: 45 minutes + cooling time

The small rounds of pearl couscous are in fact tiny balls of toasted pasta dough. Pasta pearls! They're delicious in warm dishes as well as in salads. Pearl couscous is often combined with chickpeas, but in summer I like to substitute fava beans. Let the couscous cool if you prefer your salad at room temperature. Great with Turkish pide (flatbread).

PEARL COUSCOUS WITH FAVA BEANS
and cilantro salsa verde, orange, and smoked almonds

SERVES 4

1 ¾ cups (250 grams) pearl couscous

2 shallots

8 tablespoons extra-virgin olive oil

4 cups (450 grams) fava beans (fresh or frozen)

⅓ cup (75 ml) dry white wine

1 bunch of cilantro

1 small garlic clove

2 teaspoons capers

1 tablespoon lemon juice or white wine vinegar

2 oranges

½ cup (75 grams) smoked almonds

- food processor or immersion blender with chopper attachment

COOK the couscous according to the package directions.

FINELY CHOP the shallots. Heat 3 tablespoons olive oil in a frying pan. Fry the shallot for 1 minute. Stir in the fava beans. Add the wine and cook the beans for 6–8 minutes until just tender.

PROCESS the cilantro in the food processor or chopper along with the garlic, capers, and 5 tablespoons olive oil into a smooth green sauce. Add the lemon juice or wine vinegar.

SCRUB the oranges and grate off the orange zest. Coarsely chop the almonds.

DRAIN the pearl couscous and stir it into the fava beans. Then stir the salsa verde into the couscous along with the orange zest and almonds. Season with salt and pepper.

Preparation time: 30 minutes

BEAN SPROUT OMELET
with sweet-and-sour ginger
sauce and shiitake mushrooms

RISOTTO Arborio is the best rice variety for risotto. The small round grains perfectly absorb both liquid and flavor. They also retain their bite, resulting in a risotto that's creamy, but never mushy.

TRUFFLE RISOTTO
with mushrooms and mini burrata

I love a thick omelet, especially with this filling of crispy bean sprouts. I also often use leeks or leftover cooked vegetables. Make the refreshing ginger and lime sauce and stir-fry the shiitake while the omelet cooks in the oven. Serve with white rice or noodles.

BEAN SPROUT OMELET

with sweet-and-sour ginger sauce and shiitake mushrooms

SERVES 4

4 tablespoons sunflower oil

1 cup (200 grams) bean sprouts

8 eggs

1 teaspoon ground coriander

a ¾ inch (2-cm) piece of fresh ginger

1 garlic clove

1 red bell pepper

1 can tomato paste (2 ½ ounces/70 grams)

¼ cup (50 ml) ginger syrup

juice of 1 lime

1 ½ cups (200 grams) shiitake mushrooms

1 green onion

- ovenproof pan or greased baking dish

PREHEAT the oven to 400°F (200°C). Heat 2 tablespoons oil in the ovenproof pan, then fry the bean sprouts for 2 minutes. Meanwhile, beat the eggs with the coriander and salt and pepper.

POUR the beaten eggs over the bean sprouts in the ovenproof pan or baking dish. Bake the omelet in the preheated oven for about 15 minutes until cooked through and golden brown.

PEEL and grate the ginger. Grate or press the garlic. Slice the bell pepper into thin strips.

HEAT 1 tablespoon oil in a frying pan. Fry the ginger and garlic for 1 minute. Add the bell pepper and tomato paste and fry 1 minute more.

POUR in the ginger syrup, 125 ml water, and the lime juice, and bring the sauce to a boil. Turn down the heat to low and heat gently for 8 minutes.

MEANWHILE clean the shiitake mushrooms with a brush, and cut any large ones in half. Heat 1 tablespoon oil in a wok, then stir-fry the shiitakes for 5 minutes until just done. Slice the green onion on the diagonal into rings.

TAKE the omelet out of the oven and cut into wedges. Place the wedges onto a platter, and spoon over the sweet-and-sour sauce. Top with the shiitake and sprinkle with the green onion.

Preparation time: 25 minutes

Baking time: 15 minutes

This is a luxurious, festive risotto: an assortment of mushrooms paired with earthy truffle and creamy burrata. A visual and culinary feast!

TRUFFLE RISOTTO
with mushrooms and mini burrata

SERVES 4

2 shallots

¼ cup (50 grams) butter

1 ½ cup (300 grams) risotto rice

1 ¾ cups (400 ml) red wine

3 ¼ cup (750 ml) hot vegetable stock

1 pound (500 grams) assorted mushrooms

3 sprigs of tarragon

1 garlic clove

2 tablespoons olive oil

½ cup (80 grams) truffle tapenade

4 balls of mini burrata cheese (50 grams each)

CHOP the shallots finely. Melt ⅛ cup (25 grams) butter in a heavy-bottomed pan. Fry the shallot for 1 minute. Stir in the rice, and fry gently until the grains are shiny and translucent.

POUR in half of the wine and allow the rice to absorb the wine as it gently cooks. Pour in the remaining wine and repeat, allowing the rice to gradually absorb this second quantity of wine. Stir frequently.

ADD the stock in 2 parts. Allow the rice to absorb the stock before adding the second half. Cook the rice in this way for about 20 minutes, until tender but still firm. Continue to stir frequently.

CLEAN the mushrooms with a brush and cut or tear them into pieces. Finely chop the tarragon. Grate the garlic.

HEAT the olive oil in a frying pan. Fry the mushrooms for 3 minutes. Add the garlic and tarragon and fry for another 1–2 minutes. Season with salt and pepper.

REMOVE the risotto from the heat. Stir in the rest of the of the butter, the truffle tapenade, and two-thirds of the mushrooms. Season with salt and pepper.

SPOON the risotto onto 4 plates and top with the burrata and the remaining mushrooms.

Preparation time: 30 minutes

The oven heat makes
feta softer and more
intense in taste.

Roasted feta, known as feta fourno in Greece, is a delightful creation. The heat of the oven softens the feta, intensifies the flavor, and also gives the cheese a gorgeous golden-brown hue. Try it with potatoes pan-fried in olive oil and a Greek salad.

ROASTED FETA

with olives, lemon honey, and thyme

SERVES 4

6 ounces (200 grams) feta cheese

½ cup (100 grams) olives (with pits)

1 tablespoon olive oil

1 teaspoon dried oregano

1 lemon

1 tablespoon liquid honey

1 sprig of (lemon) thyme

- baking sheet with parchment paper

PREHEAT the oven to 450°F (220°C). Place the feta on the baking sheet and arrange the olives around the cheese. Drizzle with the olive oil and sprinkle with the oregano.

ROAST the feta in the preheated oven for about 15 minutes until golden brown.

MEANWHILE scrub the lemon and grate off 1 tablespoon of the yellow zest. Mix the lemon zest with the honey, 1–2 teaspoons lemon juice, and the leaves from the thyme sprig.

TAKE the feta out of the oven and drizzle with the lemon honey and thyme.

Preparation time: 10 minutes

Baking time: 15 minutes

The dried mushrooms add an intensely savory note to the tomato sauce. Layered with creamy béchamel sauce with Parmesan cheese, the result is a firm, beautifully structured lasagna. Slice, serve, and enjoy this new family favorite!

MUSHROOM LASAGNA
with Parmesan béchamel sauce

SERVES 4

¼ cup (30 grams) dried mushrooms

2 ½ cups (250 grams) chestnut (cremini) mushrooms

1 ½ cups (200 grams) shiitake

1 onion

2 garlic cloves

2 tablespoons olive oil

6 sprigs of thyme

1 ¼ cups (250 grams) cherry tomatoes

½ cup (100 ml) red wine

4 cups (900 ml) passata (sieved tomatoes)

½ cup (50 grams) butter

⅓ cup (50 grams) flour

2 ¼ cups (500 ml) milk

¼ cup (50 grams) Parmesan cheese

1 pound (250 grams) fresh lasagna sheets

2 balls of (buffalo) mozzarella (4 ½ ounces/125 grams each)

- baking dish 8 x 11 inches (20 x 30 cm)

COARSELY chop the dried mushrooms and put them into a bowl. Pour in enough hot water to just cover the mushrooms.

CLEAN the fresh mushrooms with a brush and cut them into 1 ½ -cm pieces. Finely chop the onion and mince the garlic.

HEAT the olive oil in a frying pan. Fry the onion with the garlic and the leaves from 4 of the thyme sprigs for 1 minute. Add the mushrooms and the shiitakes and fry for another 4 minutes.

STIR in the tomatoes and fry 3 minutes more. Add the wine and the dried mushrooms along with their soaking liquid. Stir in the passata. Allow the sauce to simmer for another 10 minutes.

MEANWHILE preheat the oven to 400°F (200°C). To make the béchamel sauce, melt the butter in a saucepan. Add the flour and cook for 1 minute. Gradually whisk in the milk, allowing it to thicken into a smooth sauce.

GRATE the Parmesan cheese. Add half of the Parmesan to the béchamel sauce. Season with salt and pepper.

SPOON a layer of mushroom sauce into the baking dish. Cover with 3 lasagna sheets, and spoon on ⅓ of the mushroom sauce and 2 tablespoons béchamel sauce. Cover with 3 lasagna sheets. Repeat for all the layers. Finish with a layer of béchamel sauce.

TEAR the mozzarella into pieces and arrange them on top of the béchamel. Sprinkle with the rest of the Parmesan, the leaves of the remaining 2 thyme sprigs, and pepper to taste.

BAKE the lasagna for 30 minutes until golden brown.

Preparation time: 40 minutes

Baking time: 30 minutes

After taking the lasagna out of the oven, allow it to rest for 5 minutes, then cut into generous pieces.

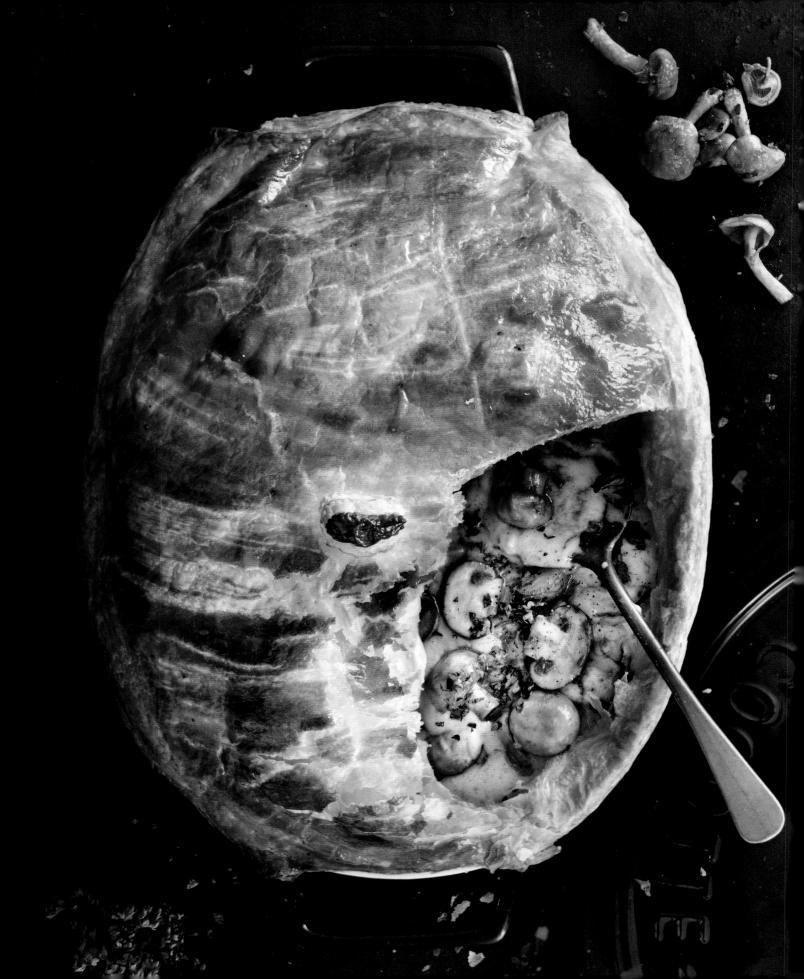

This thick and creamy homemade mushroom filling is great in vol-au-vents or on toast, but it looks particularly festive topped with a pie crust. I like to use a mix of chestnut mushrooms, king oyster mushrooms, shiitakes, and enoki mushrooms, but you can choose your own favorites.

CREAMY MUSHROOM POTPIE
with Riesling

SERVES 4

2 all-butter frozen puff
pastry sheets
2 shallots
6 cups (750 grams)
assorted mushrooms
1 cup (100 grams) butter
½ cup (75 grams) flour
¾ cup (200 ml) dry Riesling
(white wine)
2 cups (400 ml) whipping
cream
1 cup (250 ml) vegetable or
mushroom stock
2 sprigs of parsley
2 garlic cloves
1 egg yolk
- baking dish 8 x 11 inches
(20 x 30 cm or 24 cm)

PREHEAT the oven to 400°F (200°C). Allow the puff pastry to thaw at room temperature.

FINELY CHOP the shallots. Clean the mushrooms with a brush and cut them into pieces. Melt ¼ cup (25 grams butter) in a frying pan. Fry the shallot for 1 minute. Add the mushrooms and fry them for another 6 minutes.

MELT the remaining ¾ cup (75 grams) butter in a saucepan. Add the flour and cook for 1 minute, but don't allow it to brown.

REDUCE the heat to low. Slowly whisk in the wine, followed by the whipping cream and stock. Whisk until you have a thick, smooth sauce. Allow the sauce to simmer gently for 3 minutes. Finely chop the parsley.

GRATE or press the garlic into the mushrooms and fry 1 minute more. Pour in the cream sauce, add the parsley, and season with salt and pepper.

STACK the puff pastry sheets and roll them into a piece that is 1 inch (2 cm) larger than the size of the baking dish.

SPOON the creamy mushrooms into the baking dish. Brush the edge of the baking dish with egg yolk. Place the piece of puff pastry over the baking dish and press down firmly on the rim. Brush a thin layer of egg yolk onto the dough.

PLACE the baking dish in the middle of the preheated oven and bake for 20–25 minutes until the pastry is crisp and golden brown.

Preparation time: 40 minutes
Baking time: 30 minutes

Portobellos are extra-large chestnut mushrooms, often measuring 4-5 inches in diameter. They're ideal for stuffing! To me, the combination of goat cheese, spinach, and onion jam is unbeatable. I recommend Gorgonzola if you like a stronger flavor, Camembert if you prefer something milder. I like to serve these portobellos with a mix of white and wild rice.

PORTOBELLO MUSHROOMS
with spinach, goat cheese, and easy onion jam

SERVES 4

3 onions
3 tablespoons olive oil
1 ¼ cup (150 ml) ruby (red) port
½ cup (75 grams) pectin
1 ¾ cups (100 grams) semi-dried tomatoes
4 portobello mushrooms
2 garlic cloves
⅔ pound (300 grams) spinach
1 ½ cups (125 grams) soft goat cheese
- jar with a lid, immersion blender, baking dish

SLICE the onions into thin half-moons. Heat 1 tablespoon olive oil in a saucepan. Fry the onions for 6–8 minutes until soft. Add the port and the pectin and bring to a boil. Allow the jam to bubble vigorously for 2 minutes.

REMOVE the pan from the heat. Spoon the jam into a clean jar and allow to cool. Close with the lid and keep in the refrigerator.

PURÉE the tomatoes with the immersion blender until smooth or leave them a little chunkier if you prefer.

PREHEAT the oven to 400°F (200°C). Clean the portobellos with a brush and place them in the baking dish, rounded side down. Fill them with the puréed tomatoes.

MINCE the garlic. Heat 2 tablespoons olive oil in a frying pan. Fry the garlic for 1 minute. Add the spinach in 2 or 3 batches and stir-fry until the spinach is just wilted and the liquid has evaporated.

CRUMBLE the goat cheese coarsely and stir into the spinach. Season with pepper.

DIVIDE the spinach mixture over the portobellos. Bake the mushrooms in the preheated oven for 20 minutes until cooked through and brown.

TOP each portobello with a spoonful of onion jam and serve.

Preparation time: 30 minutes + cooling time
Baking time: 20 minutes

If you've got a taste for both sweet and salty and you're pressed for time, this is the recipe for you. Sriracha is a fiery Thai chili sauce that gives dishes a delightful kick.

SHIITAKE MUSHROOMS
with ginger, sriracha, and green onion

SERVES 2

¾ cup (150 grams) jasmine rice

1 teaspoon sesame seeds

2 shallots

1 ½ cups (200 grams) shiitake mushrooms

a 1-inch (2-cm) piece of fresh ginger

2 garlic cloves

2 green onions

1 tablespoon sunflower oil

3 tablespoons rice vinegar

3 tablespoons soy sauce

2 teaspoons ginger syrup

2–3 teaspoons sriracha

COOK the rice according to the package directions. Toast the sesame seeds in a dry frying pan until golden brown, then turn them onto a plate.

SLICE the shallots into thin slivers. Clean the shiitakes with a brush. Peel and grate the ginger. Grate or press the garlic. Slice the green onions into strips 1-1 ¼ inch (2–3 cm) long.

HEAT the oil in a wok. Stir the shallot into the oil, then add the shiitakes and stir-fry for 1 minute over high heat.

STIR the ginger and garlic into the shiitakes. Turn down the heat to low. Add the rice vinegar, soy sauce, and ginger syrup. Season with the sriracha.

STIR the green onion into the shiitakes at the last minute— that way they'll stay crisp. Spoon the rice into 2 bowls. Divide the shiitake mixture between the bowls, and sprinkle with the sesame seeds.

Preparation time: 20 minutes

SWEET-AND-SOUR CUCUCMBERS I like to serve this with a refreshing salad such as these cucumber "pickles." Heat 100 ml rice vinegar with 2 teaspoons sugar, stirring until the sugar is dissolved. Allow this marinade to cool to room temperature. Stir in strips or slices of cucumber and allow to marinate for an hour or longer. The flavor gets milder and the texture softer the longer the cucumber marinates.

GARDEN PEAS AND CAPUCHINS In the shell, garden peas and capuchins are easy to distinguish because garden peas have a fresh green pod while capuchins have purple pods. But, once shelled both are round and green. Both are slightly sweet when picked unripe because the seeds still contain plenty of sugars that have not yet been converted into starch. After cooking, capuchins become dented and are slightly lighter in color. Do not cook peas and capuchins for too long, they taste best with a crunchy bite!

Freshly podded peas are nice and sweet with a crunchy bite. When they're not in season, or you're pressed for time, use ½ cup (200 grams) frozen green peas and cook them until tender, about 1 minute, and certainly no longer than 2 minutes.

SPAGHETTI WITH PURPLE-PODDED PEAS
and cream, Parmesan, and lemon

SERVES 2

500 grams fresh purple-podded (capuchin) peas in the pod

1 lemon

7 ounces (200 grams) spaghetti

1 cup (200 ml) whipping cream

2 tablespoons dry white wine

¼ cup of grated Parmesan cheese

2 tablespoons basil leaves

SHELL the peas. Scrub the lemon and grate off the yellow zest.

COOK the spaghetti al dente in plenty of salted water. Cook the peas for 4–5 minutes until just tender, then drain.

PLACE the whipping cream in a saucepan and bring just to a boil. Allow the cream to cook gently for 2–3 minutes until it has reduced slightly. Turn down the heat to low. Add the wine, Parmesan, peas, and lemon zest.

DRAIN the spaghetti and mix with the cream mixture. Season with salt and pepper

DIVIDE the spaghetti over 2 plates and sprinkle with the basil leaves. Serve with a bowl of extra grated Parmesan.

Preparation time: 30 minutes

Capuchins taste
slightly sweet when
picked early.

Many cheeses taste delicious smoked, especially mozzarella. Let the smoker cool completely to prevent the mozzarella from melting. Smoking in cold smoke takes longer but imparts a subtle aroma that perfectly complements the delicate buffalo mozzarella. Smoked mozzarella is a surprise in an otherwise familiar caprese salad, but also pairs well with the harissa couscous with roast vegetables from page 31.

SMOKED BUFFALO MOZZARELLA

BASIC RECIPE
1 ball of buffalo mozzarella
(6 ounces/150 grams)
a handful of pea shoots or
arugula
extra-virgin olive oil
- an old roasting pan,
aluminum foil, 1 tablespoon
smoking dust (such as
walnut or oak)

PLACE a piece of aluminum foil on the bottom of the roasting pan. Sprinkle the smoking dust onto the foil. Take another piece of foil and fold it into a tray—you will put the mozzarella into this later. Poke holes in this tray with a skewer and place it on top of the smoking dust.

COVER the roasting pan (still without the mozzarella at this point) with a third piece of aluminum foil. Fold the foil over the rim of the pan and seal tightly so that no smoke can escape. Use another piece of foil if necessary.

PLACE the roasting pan over high heat, and heat for about 5 minutes until you start to smell the smoke. Heat for 1 minute more over low heat, then remove the pan from the heat. Allow the sealed roasting pan with the smoking dust to cool completely.

CAREFULLY open the aluminum foil and place the buffalo mozzarella in the foil tray. Tightly seal the roasting pan again and set aside for at least 1 hour to allow the mozzarella to absorb the aroma of smoke. The longer the mozzarella is exposed to the smoke aroma, the more intense the flavor will be.

SERVE the smoked buffalo mozzarella on the pea shoots or arugula, drizzled with extra-virgin olive oil.

Preparation time: 10 minutes + cooling time
Waiting time: 1–2 hours

The name tagine is used for both the conical earthenware pot and the stews that are cooked in it. Tagines have a long history, and the possibilities for the stew are endless. Tagines will often simmer away for hours, but by using canned legumes you can have your dish on the table in no time. You can even put tagines on the barbecue. No tagine? A sauté pan or a Dutch oven or heavy-bottomed pan will do just fine. Great with flatbread or couscous.

LENTIL AND BEAN TAGINE
with cherry tomatoes and lime-infused yogurt

SERVES 4

2 onions

3 garlic cloves

2 ½ cups (500 grams) cherry tomatoes

2 tablespoons olive oil

2 teaspoons turmeric

2 teaspoons cumin seeds

1 ¼ cup (250 grams) canned lentils

1 ¼ cup (250 grams) canned cannellini beans

¾ cups (150 grams) pitted green olives

½ cup (150 grams) Greek yogurt

1 lime

1 bunch of flat-leaf parsley

SLICE the onions into rings. Mince 2 of the garlic cloves. Cut the cherry tomatoes in half.

HEAT the olive oil in a tagine, Dutch oven, or heavy-bottomed pan. Fry the onion and the minced garlic for 2 minutes. Add the turmeric and cumin seeds and fry 1 minute more.

STIR in the tomatoes. Add ½ cup (150 ml) water and bring to a boil. Turn down the heat to low, cover with the (conical) lid, and simmer for 15 minutes.

STIR in the lentils, cannellini beans, and olives, then cover and simmer for another 10 minutes. Season the tagine with salt and pepper.

GRATE or press the third garlic clove into the yogurt. Scrub the lime and grate off the green zest. Add the lime zest and 1–2 tablespoons of the lime juice to the yogurt.

COARSELY chop the parsley. Serve the tagine straight from the pan or spoon it onto a platter. Sprinkle with the parsley and serve with the lime-infused yogurt.

Preparation time: 15 minutes

Cooking time: 25 minutes

LENTIL RAGU
with red wine and basil

PESTO I always make myself—no store-bought pesto comes even close! Using an immersion blender, combine 1 cup of basil leaves, 1 garlic clove, 6–7 tablespoons extra-virgin olive oil, and 1 tablespoon pine nuts. Stir in 3 heaping teaspoons grated Parmesan and season with pepper.

TAGLIATELLE WITH SPINACH
cannellini beans and pesto

This pasta sauce is ideal for weekdays when you want a quick but tasty and nutritious meal. You can do most of it the day before or earlier in the day, so when dinner comes around, all you need to do is stir in the lentils and warm them through. Serve with lots of grated Parmesan.

LENTIL RAGU
with red wine and basil

SERVES 4

1 onion

2 garlic cloves

2 celery stalks

2 ½ cups (500 grams) diced tomatoes

2 tablespoons olive oil

1 can tomato paste (2 ½ ounces/70 grams)

⅔ cup (150 ml) red wine

12 ounces (350 grams) spaghetti

1 ¼ cup (250 grams) canned lentils

a handful of basil leaves

Parmesan cheese

CHOP the onion finely. Mince the garlic. Slice the celery into arches and dice the tomatoes.

HEAT the olive oil in a frying pan. Fry the onion with the garlic and celery for 2 minutes. Stir in the tomatoes and fry 4 minutes more. Add the tomato paste along with the wine and ½ cup (150 ml) water, then bring the sauce to a boil.

REDUCE the heat to low and simmer for 15 minutes, stirring occasionally. Meanwhile, cook the spaghetti al dente.

DRAIN the spaghetti. Stir the lentils into the sauce and season with salt and pepper.

MIX the spaghetti with the sauce and spoon onto a platter or 4 plates. Sprinkle with the basil leaves. Grate on a generous amount of Parmesan cheese at the table.

Preparation time: 25 minutes

I could eat beans morning, noon, and night. Sometimes I'll even spoon them straight out of the can. The quality of canned beans—which are steamed inside their cans—has improved a lot in recent years, but I like the full flavor and bite of dried beans that are soaked and cooked at home. It's not complicated, but it does take more time. This recipe uses canned beans, because on weekdays it's nice to serve up a quick, healthy, and nutritious pasta dish.

TAGLIATELLE WITH SPINACH
cannellini beans and pesto

SERVES 4

14 ounces (400 grams) tagliatelle

2 garlic cloves

2 tablespoons olive oil

1 pound (600 grams) spinach

18 ounces (500 grams) canned cannellini beans

3 tablespoons basil pesto

Parmesan cheese, to serve

COOK the tagliatelle al dente in plenty of salted water. Mince the garlic.

HEAT the olive oil in a large frying pan. Fry the garlic for 1 minute. Add the spinach in 2 or 3 batches and stir-fry until just wilted. Rinse the beans, add them to the spinach, and heat for 1 minute more.

DRAIN the tagliatelle. Mix the noodles and the pesto into the spinach and cannellini beans. Season with pepper and divide over 4 plates. Grate on a generous amount of Parmesan cheese at the table.

Preparation time: 15 minutes

Growing up, I was never a big fan of canned beans in tomato sauce. In my grown-up version of this dish, I like to use giant white beans and garlic, rosemary, and coriander seeds for a bit of a savory kick. Serve in the pan along with a few slices of toast, so that not a drop of sauce is wasted. It's easy to scale up the ingredients for more people.

GIANT WHITE BEANS IN TOMATO SAUCE
with red wine, coriander seeds, and rosemary

SERVES 2

3 garlic cloves

2 sprigs of rosemary

2 teaspoons coriander seeds

1 ½ cups (200 grams) button mushrooms

6 tablespoons olive oil

⅔ cup (150 ml) red wine

1 cup (250 ml) passata (sieved tomatoes)

12 ounces (350 grams) canned giant white beans or butter beans

4 slices of sourdough bread

- mortar and pestle (optional)

FINELY CHOP the garlic and the needles from the rosemary sprigs. Crush the coriander seeds in the mortar or with the flat of a knife. Clean the mushrooms with a brush.

HEAT 3 tablespoons olive oil in a frying pan. Fry the garlic with the rosemary and the coriander seeds for 1 minute.

ADD the mushrooms and fry for 3 minutes more. Pour in the wine and allow to simmer for another 3–4 minutes.

ADD the passata and bring to a boil. Turn down the heat to low. Add the giant white beans and allow to simmer gently for another 8 minutes.

MEANWHILE add the remaining 3 tablespoons olive oil to a second frying pan. Fry the bread on both sides until crisp and golden brown. Sprinkle the toast lightly with salt.

SERVE the beans along with the toast.

Preparation time: 30 minutes

This creamy bean purée is great when you fancy a change from mashed potatoes. I like it best when it's silky smooth and still a bit liquid. If the purée is too thick to your liking, you can add some extra wine or water.

CANNELLINI BEAN PURÉE
with crème fraiche

SERVES 2–3

18 ounces (500 grams) canned cannellini beans

1 garlic clove

2 tablespoons olive oil

⅔ cup (150 ml) dry white wine

½ cup (125 ml) crème fraiche

2 sprigs of thyme

extra-virgin olive oil

- food processor or immersion blender

RINSE the beans in a sieve and allow them to drain well. Mince the garlic.

HEAT the olive oil in a frying pan. Fry the garlic for 1 minute. Stir in the beans. Pour in the wine and gently heat the beans for 5 minutes until they're hot.

SPOON the beans into the food processor or tall measuring cup along with the cooking liquid. Process into a smooth purée.

STIR the crème fraiche into the hot purée and season with pepper.

SPOON the purée into a serving dish. Sprinkle with the leaves from the thyme sprigs, and drizzle with a little more extra-virgin olive oil.

Preparation time: 20 minutes

Chickpeas are among my favorite legumes. They're versatile and high in fiber and protein. I particularly like their full, nutty flavor and always have a few cans on hand to add to a salad or a pasta sauce. They're great in stews, too. Bulgur (crushed or cracked wheat) is lovely with this, as is couscous, rice, pita bread, or flatbread.

CHICKPEA STEW
with Romano peppers and dates

SERVES 4

1 onion

2 red Romano (sweet pointed) peppers

3 tablespoons olive oil

1 teaspoon ground cumin

½ teaspoon ground cinnamon

1 teaspoon chili powder (ground chiles)

1 bottle passata (sieved tomatoes, 24 ounces/ 690 grams)

1 ¼ cup (250 grams) Bulgur

10-13 (125 grams) pitted dates

18 ounces (500 grams) canned chickpeas

2 sprigs of mint

FINELY CHOP the onion. Cut the peppers into pieces 1 ¼–2 inches (3–4 cm) wide.

HEAT the olive oil in a Dutch oven or heavy-bottomed pan. Fry the onion for 2 minutes. Stir in the cumin, cinnamon, and chili powder and fry gently for 1 minute more.

STIR in the peppers. Add the passata along with ⅔ cup (150 ml) water and bring to a boil. Turn down the heat to low, cover with the lid, and allow the tomato sauce to simmer for 20 minutes.

COOK the bulgur according to the package directions. Cut the dates into chunks.

STIR the chickpeas and the dates into the tomato sauce, then put the lid back on and simmer for another 10 minutes.

SEASON the chickpea stew with salt and pepper. Sprinkle with the mint leaves and serve with the bulgur.

Preparation time: 15 minutes

Cooking time: 30 minutes

Chickpeas are my go-to legume in this fiery curry, but lentils and beans are good too.

THAI RED CURRY WITH CHICKPEAS
ginger and cilantro

SERVES 4

2 shallots

2 garlic cloves

a 1 ¼ inch (3-cm) piece of fresh ginger

2 red Romano (sweet pointed) peppers

2 tablespoons oil

2 tablespoons Thai red curry paste

1 can coconut milk (15 ounces/400 ml)

250 grams rice noodles

1 ½ cups (200 grams) peas (frozen)

9 ounces (250 grams) canned chickpeas

1 bunch cilantro

CHOP the shallots finely. Mince the garlic. Peel and finely grate the ginger. Cut the peppers into strips.

HEAT the oil in a frying pan. Fry the shallots with the garlic and ginger for 1 minute. Add the curry paste and fry 1 minute more. Stir in the pepper strips.

POUR in the coconut milk and bring just to a boil. Allow to simmer gently for 4–5 minutes until it has reduced to a sauce.

COOK the rice noodles according to the package directions. Thaw the peas in a sieve under warm running water, then drain well.

ADD the chickpeas and the peas to the curry and heat for another 2 minutes. Coarsely chop the cilantro.

DIVIDE the rice noodles over 4 plates. Spoon the curry alongside the noodles and sprinkle with the cilantro.

Preparation time: 20 minutes

WHOLE-WHEAT LASAGNA WITH LENTILS
and mozzarella crème

**CHICKPEAS
WITH SPINACH**
in vadouvan sauce

Lentils, which are high in iron and plant proteins, are a common ingredient in many Mediterranean stews and salads. The many different types vary hugely in flavor and structure: from rich and earthy to sweet and nutty, and from silky soft to firm. I often sprinkle them into a green salad or a soup, and I also use them in everyday dishes like the lentil ragu from page 144 and in this recipe, one of my family's favorite lasagnas.

WHOLE-WHEAT LASAGNA WITH LENTILS
and mozzarella crème

SERVES 4

1 onion

2 garlic cloves

2 tablespoons olive oil

1 teaspoon chili flakes

2 teaspoons dried oregano

(2 ½ ounces/70 grams) tomato paste

2 15-ounce (400-gram) cans diced tomatoes

9 ounces (250 grams) canned lentils

4 ½ ounces (125 grams) crème fraiche

1 ball of mozzarella (4 ½ ounces/125 grams)

¼ cup (25 grams) Parmesan cheese

9 ounces (250 grams) fresh or no-boil whole-wheat lasagna sheets

- baking dish 8 x 11 inch (20 x 30 cm)

CHOP the onion finely and mince the garlic. Heat the olive oil in a frying pan. Gently fry the onion with the garlic, chili flakes, and oregano for 2 minutes.

STIR in the tomato paste and fry 1 minute more. Add the diced tomatoes along with the liquid from the can and 1 cup (200 ml) water. Bring just to a boil. Sprinkle in the lentils and allow the sauce to cook gently for 10 minutes. Season with salt and pepper.

STIR the crème fraiche. Tear the mozzarella into small pieces. Grate the Parmesan cheese. Stir the mozzarella and Parmesan into the crème fraiche. Add pepper to taste.

SPOON a layer of lentil sauce into the baking dish and cover with 3 lasagna sheets. Then spoon on another thin layer of sauce and top with 3 lasagna sheets. Repeat this with the rest of the sauce and lasagna sheets. Make sure the layers of sauce are thin so that the lasagna is nice and firm. Finish with a layer of sauce. Spoon on the mozzarella crème, making sure that all of the lasagna sheets are covered.

BAKE the lasagna in the preheated oven for about 40 minutes until cooked through and golden brown. After taking the lasagna out of the oven, allow it to rest for 5 minutes, then cut into generous pieces.

Preparation time: 30 minutes

Baking time: 40 minutes

Chickpeas have a nutty flavor that I love. These chickpeas with spinach in creamy vadouvan sauce are delicious with spaghetti, rice, or bulgur, or with the flatbread from page 27. Vadouvan is a French spice mix. Inspired by garam masala, an Indian curry blend, its flavor is familiar, sophisticated, and deeply aromatic.

CHICKPEAS WITH SPINACH
in vadouvan sauce

SERVES 2

1 shallot

1 tablespoon olive oil

1 teaspoon vadouvan

¼ cup (75 ml) dry white wine

1 cup (200 ml) whipping cream

½ pound (200 grams) spinach

9 ounces (250 grams) canned chickpeas

CHOP the shallot finely. Heat the olive oil in a frying pan and fry the shallot for 3 minutes.

STIR in the vadouvan and fry just a bit longer. Add the wine and allow to reduce to 3 tablespoons. Add the whipping cream and cook for 4–5 minutes until it has thickened to a sauce.

PLUNGE the spinach into a generous amount of boiling water for 30 seconds. Transfer the spinach to a colander and drain well.

STIR the chickpeas and the spinach into the vadouvan sauce and heat for 1 minute more. Season with salt and pepper.

Preparation time: 20 minutes

Split pea soup—often served with pork sausage—is a winter classic. This vegetarian version owes its intense flavor to dried mushrooms. I grind them so their aroma really infuses the soup. For the best flavor and best consistency—the soup should be thick enough for a spoon to stand upright!—I recommend you make the pea soup a day in advance. Reheat over a low heat and, if necessary, add a cup of water.

VEGETARIAN SPLIT PEA SOUP
with dried mushrooms

SERVES 4

2 ¼ cups (500 grams) split peas

10 cups (2 ½ liters) vegetable stock

¼ cup (25 grams) dried mushrooms

1 pound (400 grams) regular potatoes or sweet potatoes

½ celery root

1 leek

5 sprigs of thyme

- immersion blender with chopper attachment

PLACE the split peas and the stock in a soup pan and bring to a boil. Finely chop the dried mushrooms in the chopper and add to the pan.

PEAL the potatoes or sweet potatoes and the celery root and dice them into 1-cm cubes. Slice the leeks into rings. Add them to the soup along with the thyme.

TURN down the heat to low and allow the split peas to cook gently for 1–1.5 hours, until they're disintegrating.

SEASON the split pea soup with salt and pepper. Cool the soup quickly, for example, by placing the pan in a sink filled with cold water. Cover and keep the soup in the refrigerator or another cool spot.

NEXT day, reheat the soup over low heat. Add an extra cup of water if necessary. To keep the soup from scorching, stir well and frequently over the bottom of the pan with a wooden spoon.

Preparation time: 15 minutes
Cooking time: 1.5 hours

EGGS IN SOY SAUCE

EGGS IN GREEN CURRY SAUCE

EGGS IN CHILI-PEANUT SAUCE

EGGS IN TOMATO-GINGER SAUCE

EGGS IN RED WINE SAUCE

EGGS IN STROGANOFF SAUCE

EGGS are a perfect ingredient for a weekday meal without meat or fish. These are a few of the recipes I like to prepare at home. Quick, simple, and above all, delicious.

Eggs and sweet soy sauce—two quintessential ingredients in Indonesian cooking. Sometimes I'll add a spoonful of honey or ginger syrup to the sauce for a milder flavor.

EGGS IN SOY SAUCE

SERVES 4

6 eggs

1 onion

2 garlic cloves

1 tablespoon sunflower oil

1 tablespoon tomato paste

¼ cup (50 ml)

sweet soy sauce

BOIL the eggs for 7 minutes until they are just hard. Meanwhile, finely chop the onion and mince the garlic.

HEAT the oil in a small frying pan. Fry the onion and garlic for 1 minute. Add the tomato paste and fry 1 minute more.

POUR in the soy sauce along with ½ cup (100 ml) water and stir until the soy-tomato sauce is smooth. Allow the sauce to simmer gently for 1 minute.

PEEL the eggs, add them to the pan, and ladle over the sauce. Season with pepper.

Preparation time: 15 minutes

As well as making my own, I also often use curry paste from a jar. My fridge is filled with curry pastes in all colors of the rainbow. They're perfect for a quick weekday meal, when I'm running behind and have a hungry family to feed. If you prefer, you can swap this Thai green curry paste for a red or yellow one. This is delicious served with stir-fried bok choy and fragrant jasmine rice.

EGGS IN GREEN CURRY SAUCE

SERVES 4

6 eggs

1 onion

1 tablespoon sunflower oil

1 tablespoon Thai green curry paste

¾ cup (200 ml) coconut milk

BOIL the eggs for 7 minutes until they are just hard. Meanwhile, finely chop the onion.

HEAT the oil in a small frying pan. Fry the onion for 1 minute. Add the curry paste and fry 1 minute more.

POUR in the coconut milk and stir until the sauce is smooth. Allow the sauce to simmer gently for 1 minute.

PEEL the eggs, add them to the pan, and ladle over the curry sauce.

Preparation time: 15 minutes

Eggs and red wine may sound like an unlikely combination, but it's a classic pairing in French cooking. One such classic dish is "oeufs en meurette": poached eggs in red wine sauce. Feel free to substitute poached eggs (see page 226) for the hard-boiled eggs in this recipe. And you could add some pan-fried, sliced mushrooms for variation.

EGGS IN RED WINE SAUCE

SERVES 4

6 eggs

2 tablespoons butter

1 tablespoon tomato paste

2 teaspoons flour

1 cup (250 ml) smooth red wine (such as Merlot)

1 bay leaf

3 sprigs of thyme

BOIL the eggs for 7 minutes until they are just hard. Meanwhile, melt the butter in a saucepan. Add the tomato paste and the flour and fry for 1 minute.

SLOWLY whisk in the wine and continue whisking until the sauce is smooth.

ADD the bay leaf and thyme. Allow the sauce to simmer gently for 6 minutes. Season with salt and pepper.

PEEL the eggs, add them to the pan, and ladle over the red wine sauce.

Preparation time: 15 minutes

This is a family favorite: eggs in a peanut sauce seasoned with sweet chili. Simple, but just right for a quick weekday meal with broccoli and flavorful white rice. I like to make my own peanut butter. For the recipe, see page 19.

EGGS IN CHILI-PEANUT SAUCE

SERVES 4

6 eggs

2 tablespoons peanut butter

4 tablespoons sweet soy sauce

¾ cup (200 ml) coconut milk

3 tablespoons sweet chili sauce

1 tablespoon grated coconut

BOIL the eggs for 7 minutes until they are just hard. Meanwhile, heat the peanut butter and the soy sauce in a saucepan for 1 minute.

POUR in the coconut milk and bring just to a boil. Heat for another 3–4 minutes, until the sauce has reached the desired thickness. Add the chili sauce and stir until smooth.

MEANWHILE toast the grated coconut in a dry frying pan until golden brown. Turn onto a plate.

PEEL the eggs, add them to the pan, and ladle over the chili-peanut sauce. Sprinkle with the coconut.

Preparation time: 15 minutes

I love the combination of tomato and ginger. While the tomato creates a mild and sweet base, the ginger injects some fire.

EGGS IN TOMATO-GINGER SAUCE

SERVES 4

6 eggs

a 1 ¼ inch (3-cm) piece of fresh ginger

1 garlic clove

1 tablespoon olive oil

15 ounces (400 grams) diced tomatoes

a handful of basil leaves

- immersion blender

BOIL the eggs for 7 minutes until they are just hard. Meanwhile, peel and finely grate the ginger. Mince the garlic.

HEAT the olive oil in a saucepan. Fry the ginger and garlic for 1 minute.

PLACE the diced tomatoes into a tall measuring cup and purée with the immersion blender. Pour the puréed tomatoes into the pan, and gently heat the sauce for 5 minutes.

PEEL the eggs, add them to the pan, and gently ladle over the tomato-ginger sauce. Sprinkle with the basil leaves.

Preparation time: 15 minutes

Stroganoff sauce has its origins in Russia and was named after the Stroganov family and for that reason alone, a splash of vodka wouldn't go amiss. If you don't have vodka, you can use white wine or brandy instead.

EGGS IN STROGANOFF SAUCE

SERVES 4

6 eggs

1 onion

1 small red bell pepper

3 ½ ounces (100 grams) cremini mushrooms

1 tablespoon olive oil

2 ½ ounces (70 grams) tomato paste

1 teaspoon paprika

1 ½ ounce (50 ml) vodka

½ cup (125 ml) whipping cream

1 sprig of parsley

BOIL the eggs for 7 minutes until they are just hard. Meanwhile, finely chop the onion. Cut the bell pepper into thin strips and the mushrooms into slices.

HEAT the olive oil in a frying pan. Fry the onion with the bell pepper and the mushrooms for 4 minutes.

ADD the tomato paste and the paprika and fry 1 minute more. Pour in the vodka and stir until smooth.

ADD the whipping cream and gently simmer the sauce for another 1–2 minutes. Season with pepper. Finely chop the parsley.

PEEL the eggs, add them to the pan, and gently ladle over the stroganoff sauce. Sprinkle with the parsley.

Preparation time: 15 minutes

Who doesn't love creamed spinach? It's a classic for a good reason. This recipe is going to be a favorite, I can guarantee you. It's as easy to make for four people as it is for two. Just double the ingredients and use a bigger casserole dish. Great with pan-fried or roasted potato wedges or skin-on baby potatoes.

CRUNCHY BAKED SPINACH
with cream, Emmentaler, and lemon

SERVES 2

1 pound (600 grams) spinach

2 garlic cloves

1 onion

1 tablespoon olive oil

½ cup (100 ml) whipping cream

2 slices white sandwich bread

1 ¼ cups (100 grams) grated Emmentaler or similar Swiss cheese

½ lemon

- food processor or immersion blender with chopper attachment, greased baking dish (750 ml)

PREHEAT the oven to 400°F (200°C). Wash the spinach and remove any hard stems. Cook the spinach in plenty of water for 1 minute. Tip into a colander and allow to drain well.

MINCE 1 garlic clove and finely chop the onion. Heat ½ tablespoon olive oil in a frying pan. Fry the onion with the minced garlic for 3 minutes, but don't allow it to brown. Pour in the whipping cream and cook until it has reduced by half.

CUT the crusts off of the bread and process the slices into fine breadcrumbs in the food processor or chopper. Put the breadcrumbs into a bowl. Scrub the lemon and grate the yellow zest into the bowl. Grate or press in the other garlic clove.

MIX the breadcrumbs with half of the cheese and ½ tablespoon olive oil. Add salt and pepper to taste.

STIR the rest of the Swiss cheese into the hot cream along with the spinach. Season with salt and pepper. Spoon everything into the baking dish and top with the breadcrumb-cheese mixture.

BAKE the spinach casserole in the preheated oven for 10–15 minutes until golden brown and crunchy.

Preparation time: 20 minutes
Baking time: 10-15 minutes

Polenta is as popular in Italy as mashed potatoes are in many other parts of the world. Polenta is made by grinding dried corn into flour or meal. Although it's usually cooked into a kind of savory porridge, it's also often used in cookies and cakes. This casserole has two layers of savory polenta around a spinach filling. After topping with Gorgonzola and pine nuts, the dish goes back in the oven for a few minutes, until the cheese melts and bubbles and the pine nuts turn golden and fragrant.

POLENTA AND SPINACH GRATIN
with Gorgonzola and pine nuts

SERVES 4

1 ¾ cups (250 grams) polenta
2 celery stalks
2 garlic cloves
4 tablespoons olive oil
1 ⅓ pounds (600 grams) spinach
½ cup (125 ml) milk
5 ½ ounces (150 grams) Gorgonzola
2 tablespoons pine nuts
- greased baking dish
8 x 11 inch (20 x 30 cm)

BOIL 5 cups (about 1 liter) water along with 1 tablespoon salt. While stirring, sprinkle the polenta into the boiling water. Gently cook the polenta for 10 minutes into a thick porridge. Stir frequently and watch out for splatters!

MEANWHILE preheat the oven to 450°F (220°C). Slice the celery into arches and mince the garlic. Heat 2 tablespoons olive oil in a frying pan. Fry the celery and garlic for 1 minute.

ADD the spinach in batches and stir-fry until the spinach is just wilted and the liquid has evaporated. Season with salt and pepper.

REMOVE the polenta from the heat. Stir in the milk and a little pepper; salt is probably no longer needed.

SPOON half of the polenta into the baking dish. Add the spinach in an even layer, then spoon on the rest of the polenta. Cut the Gorgonzola into slices and distribute them over the polenta along with the pine nuts. Drizzle with 2 tablespoons olive oil, and sprinkle with a little more pepper.

PUT the polenta casserole into the preheated oven for 10 minutes until the cheese is melted and lightly browned.

Preparation time: 20 minutes
Baking time: 10 minutes

SKILLET QUICHE
WITH LEAFY GREEN
VEGETABLES
ricotta and Parmesan

SWISS CHARD AND POTATO MASH
with mushrooms

If you're using an ovenproof skillet, the quiche can go straight to the table. Alternatively, you can use a quiche pan or a low springform pan. I sprinkle the puff pastry with finely chopped herbs for a quick and delicious herb dough. You can also add grated lemon zest for some zing.

SKILLET QUICHE WITH LEAFY GREEN VEGETABLES
ricotta and Parmesan

SERVES 4

2 sheets frozen puff pastry or pie crust

1 pound (600 grams) leafy green vegetables (such as spinach, Swiss chard, or escarole)

2 garlic cloves

2 tablespoons olive oil

3–4 sprigs of thyme

4 eggs

½ cup (150 grams) ricotta

a generous handful of grated Parmesan cheese

- greased ovenproof skillet or quiche or pie pan

PREHEAT the oven to 400°F (200°C). Allow the puff pastry or pie crust to thaw at room temperature. Cut the leafy green vegetables into strips. Mince the garlic.

HEAT the olive oil in a frying pan. Fry the garlic for 1 minute. Add the vegetables a handful at a time and stir-fry for 5 minutes.

STRIP the leaves from the thyme sprigs.

ROLL the pastry into a circle large enough to cover the pan. Line the pan with the thyme-leaf pastry. Fold any overhanging pastry back over the rim of the pan. Distribute the vegetables over the bottom of the pastry shell.

BEAT the eggs. Mix in the ricotta, Parmesan cheese, and salt and pepper to taste. Pour the egg-cheese mixture over the vegetables.

BAKE the quiche in the preheated oven for 35-40 minutes until cooked through and golden brown.

Preparation time: 20 minutes
Baking time: 35-40 minutes

I feel Swiss chard is an underrated vegetable and perhaps not as popular as it should be. Both the leaves and the colorful stalks can be used in all kinds of recipes. I like to use chard in mashed potato dishes. If you don't overcook the chard, it adds a nice bit of crunch.

SWISS CHARD AND POTATO MASH
with mushrooms

SERVES 4

3 ⅓ pounds (1 ½ kilos) starchy potatoes

1 pound (500 grams) Swiss chard

1 pound (400 grams) assorted mushrooms

2 garlic cloves

6 tablespoons butter

1 cup (250 ml) whole milk

9 ounces (250 grams) Dutch blue cheese (or other blue cheese such as Gorgonzola or Stilton)

- potato masher or mixer

PEEL the potatoes and cut them into pieces. Cook the potatoes in salted water for 20 minutes until done.

CLEAN the Swiss chard and chop very coarsely. Clean the mushrooms with a brush and cut them into pieces. Mince the garlic.

MELT 2 tablespoons butter in a large frying pan. Stir in the chard and cook for 6–8 minutes until crisp-tender or completely tender, as desired. Next, melt 2 tablespoons butter in a second frying pan. Stir-fry the mushrooms for 4 minutes, then add the garlic and fry for another 2 minutes.

HEAT the milk with the final 2 tablespoons butter. Drain the potatoes and mash them with the milk into a creamy purée. Stir in the chard and season with salt and pepper.

SPOON the Swiss chard and potato mash onto 4 plates. Divide the fried mushrooms over the mash, and crumble on the blue cheese in small chunks. At the table, everyone can mix the mushrooms and blue cheese into their own serving of mash.

Preparation time: 30 minutes

Belgian endive used to be extremely bitter, which is why recipes often called for the addition of something sweet. Today's endive varieties are much milder, but I still like a touch of sweetness, especially in combination with the bitter note of the beer.

BELGIAN ENDIVE
with beer, honey, and thyme

SERVES 4

1 ½ pounds (800 grams) Belgian endive

2 tablespoons butter

1 generous tablespoon honey

¼ cup (50 ml) dark Trappist beer (or other dark ale)

5 sprigs of thyme

CUT a thin slice off the bottom of the heads of Belgian endive and cut the heads in half.

MELT the butter in a large frying pan. Fry the Belgian endive for 5 minutes until browned on both sides.

DRIZZLE the honey over the halves. Pour in the beer and add the thyme sprigs. Bring to a boil.

TURN down the heat to low and braise the Belgian endive until done, about 10 minutes. Don't cover the pan with a lid but allow the cooking liquid to reduce to a syrup. Turn frequently.

SEASON with pepper and arrange the Belgian endive on a platter or 4 plates. Delicious with creamy mashed potatoes.

Preparation time: 30 minutes

A baked endive dish ought to be in everybody's weekday repertoire. I make mine with walnuts, breadcrumbs, garlic, and rosemary. Serve with potatoes pan-fried in olive oil and sprinkled with a bit of sea salt.

BAKED ENDIVE
with walnuts and rosemary crumble

SERVES 4

2 ¼ pounds (1 kilo) Belgian endive and/or radicchio

2 slices white bread

9 sprigs of rosemary

1 garlic clove

2 teaspoons olive oil

8 slices Gouda or Monterey Jack cheese

¾ cup (75 grams) walnuts

- food processor or immersion blender with chopper attachment, greased baking dish 8 x 11 inch (20 x 30 cm)

PREHEAT the oven to 450°F (220°C). Cut a thin slice off the ends of the heads of Belgian endive and/or radicchio. Cook them in salted water for 8–10 minutes until just tender.

PROCESS the bread slices in the food processor or chopper with the needles of 1 rosemary sprig into fine breadcrumbs. Press or grate in the garlic and mix the olive oil and a little salt into the breadcrumbs.

DRAIN the Belgian endive and/or radicchio. Wrap a slice of cheese around each head, and tuck in the remaining rosemary sprigs. Place them in the baking dish, and top with the walnuts and rosemary breadcrumbs.

BAKE in the preheated oven for about 10 minutes, until the cheese is melted and the breadcrumbs are crunchy and golden brown.

Preparation time: 25 minutes
Baking time: 10 minutes

LEFTOVER POLENTA? Ladle the polenta onto a plate, smooth the top, and allow to cool in the refrigerator for at least two hours. Cover and store until further use. Cut the polenta neatly into pieces and grill or fry in olive oil until golden brown and crisp. Great with a fresh tomato salad.

OLIVE RAGU WITH CHERRY TOMATOES

polenta and crispy basil

TOMATO AND BELL PEPPER PAELLA
with purple-podded peas

This olive ragu is a variation on the lentil ragu from page 144. While the lentil ragu is fairly delicate and mild, this olive version has a much stronger and heartier flavor. If you love olives, this one's for you!

OLIVE RAGU WITH CHERRY TOMATOES
polenta and crispy basil

SERVES 4

1 onion

3 celery stalks

2 garlic cloves

5 tablespoons olive oil

2–3 teaspoons fennel seeds

14 ounces (400 grams) cherry tomatoes

7 ounces (200 grams) pitted black olives

1 ⅓ cup (200 grams) polenta

1 can (6 ounces/140 grams) tomato paste

½ cup (100 ml) red wine

a handful of basil leaves

⅔ cup (150 ml) milk

2 ½ ounces (75 grams) Parmesan cheese

- immersion blender with chopper attachment

CHOP the onion and the celery finely and mince the garlic. Heat 2 tablespoons olive oil in a frying pan. Fry the onion with the celery, garlic, and fennel seeds for 2 minutes.

CUT the cherry tomatoes into pieces and then add them to the onion mixture and fry for another 4 minutes.

BOIL 5 cups (1 liter) water along with 1 tablespoon salt and then sprinkle the polenta into the boiling water and cook for 10–15 minutes until done. Stir frequently and watch out for splatters!

CHOP the olives finely (I like to use the chopper for this, too) and then stir them into the vegetables and fry for 2 minutes.

STIR the tomato paste into the vegetable mixture and fry 1 minute more. Add the red wine and ⅔ cup (150 ml) water. Bring to a boil, turn down the heat to low, and allow the sauce to simmer for another 10 minutes.

HEAT 3 tablespoons olive oil in a frying pan. Fry the basil leaves for a few seconds until crisp—don't let them get too dark! Put them straight onto a plate and allow to cool.

HEAT the milk and grate the Parmesan cheese. Remove the polenta from the heat and stir in the hot milk along with half of the Parmesan. Season with salt and pepper.

SPOON the polenta into 4 deep plates. Top the polenta with the olive ragu and sprinkle with the crispy basil leaves. Serve with the rest of the Parmesan.

Preparation time: 30 minutes

I'm sure we can all picture Italian vineyards with families eating lunch at long tables. This is the Spanish equivalent: families gathered around large paella pans on a Sunday afternoon, with the size of the party determining the size of the pan. And when Spain's best-known rice dish is served, everybody digs straight in with a spoon. For me, the best thing about paella is the "socarrat," the crispy crust. To achieve it, stop stirring after you've added the last bit of the stock, so the rice sticks to the bottom of the pan and forms a crispy layer.

TOMATO AND BELL PEPPER PAELLA
with purple-podded peas

SERVES 4–6

2 pinches of saffron

6 ⅓ cups (1 ½ liters) hot vegetable stock

4 garlic cloves

2 red bell peppers

2 pounds (1 kilo) tomatoes

4 tablespoons olive oil

2 tablespoons smoked paprika

3 cups (500 grams) paella or risotto rice

¾ pound (300 grams) purple-podded (capuchin) peas, fava beans, or large lima beans (shelled; fresh, frozen, or canned)

a handful of parsley

3 lemons

SOAK the saffron in the vegetable stock. Press or grate the garlic. Slice 6 rings from the bell peppers and cut the rest into strips. Cut the tomatoes into pieces.

HEAT the olive oil in a paella pan or sauté pan. Gently fry the garlic and smoked paprika for 1 minute. Add the bell pepper strips and fry for 2 minutes.

STIR the tomato into the bell pepper mixture and fry for another 10 minutes until the tomatoes are soft, then add the rice and fry for 2 minutes until the grains of rice are translucent. Pour in half of the stock. Allow the rice to simmer gently for 8–10 minutes until the stock has been absorbed.

ADD the peas, fava or lima beans, and the rest of the stock, and bring it just back to a boil. Arrange the bell pepper rings on top of the rice and allow the paella to cook gently for another 10 minutes. If the rice cooks dry, add more stock or water, but the paella should no longer be stirred. It's fine if the rice sticks to the bottom of the pan—Spaniards just love this crunchy crust known as "socarrat."

CHOP the parsley coarsely and cut the lemons into wedges. Season the paella with salt and pepper, and sprinkle with the parsley. Serve with the lemon wedges. Put the pan on the table and add spoons. Eat it straight from the pan like they do in Spain or give everyone a plate.

Preparation time: 45 minutes

This is one of my simplest yet tastiest pasta sauces. You can use any kind of tomato—vine, cherry, beefsteak—as long as they're ripe and juicy. You can swap the ravioli for rigatoni or a ribbon pasta if you prefer. If you like a bit of heat, drizzle on a bit of chili oil to finish it.

RAVIOLI WITH TOMATO-MASCARPONE SAUCE
and basil

SERVES 4

1 ⅓ pound (600 grams) ripe tomatoes

3 tablespoons olive oil

2 garlic cloves

1 ¼ pounds (500 grams) good-quality ravioli

3 sprigs of basil

5 ounces (150 grams) mascarpone

chili oil from page 230 (optional)

CUT the tomatoes into pieces. Heat the olive oil in a frying pan. Fry the tomatoes for 5 minutes over high heat until their delicious juices are released.

GRATE or press the garlic into the tomatoes and fry 1 minute more. Meanwhile, cook the ravioli in plenty of boiling salted water for 3–4 minutes until done. Finely chop the basil leaves.

TURN down the heat to low. Stir the mascarpone and a splash of pasta water into the tomatoes to create a creamy sauce. Season with salt and pepper.

TRANSFER the ravioli to plates using a slotted spoon and then spoon on the sauce. Sprinkle with the basil and drizzle on a little chili oil if using.

Preparation time: 20 minutes

This recipe has its origins in Louisiana's Cajun cooking, where it's known as "dirty rice." The rice often has a vaguely "dirty" color, hence the name. Tomato lends a refreshing—and colorful—note to this version. It's not traditional, but I like to add a spoonful of yogurt to this aromatic dish.

CAJUN RICE
with bell pepper and tomato

SERVES 4

1 vegetable bouillon cube

1 can tomato paste
(2 ½ ounces/70 grams)

1 onion

2 garlic cloves

2 celery stalks

2 bell peppers

½ pound (250 grams) cherry tomatoes

2 tablespoons sunflower oil

2 tablespoons Cajun seasoning

2 teaspoons smoked paprika

1 ½ cups (300 grams) basmati rice

2 bay leaves

9 ounces (250 grams) canned kidney beans

1 green onion

2 sprigs of parsley

½ cup (150 grams) Greek yogurt

DISSOLVE the bouillon cube in 4 ¼ cups (1 liter) of hot water, then stir in the tomato paste.

CHOP the onion finely and mince the garlic. Slice the celery into arches and the bell peppers into thin strips. Cut the tomatoes in half.

HEAT the oil in a sauté pan. Fry the onion with the garlic and celery for 2 minutes. Add the bell pepper and fry for another 3 minutes. Stir in the Cajun seasoning and the smoked paprika and fry 1 minute more. Stir in the rice and tomatoes and fry for another 2 minutes.

POUR in 3 cups (750 ml) of the tomato bouillon. Add the bay leaves and bring to a boil. Place the lid on the pan and gently simmer the rice for 10 minutes until done. If the rice cooks dry, add a little more bouillon.

STIR the kidney beans into the rice and season with (cayenne) pepper. Cover and allow the rice to stand for 5 minutes.

SLICE the green onion into rings and finely chop the parsley. Sprinkle the green onion and parsley onto the rice and serve with the yogurt.

Preparation time: 30-40 minutes

ROASTED VEGETABLE PITHIVIERS

and Parmesan sauce

A pithivier is a pastry enclosed pie.

The full name for this impressive French puff pastry pie is "gâteau pithiviers" and it's named after a town some fifty miles south of Paris. The filling between the round layers of pastry can be either sweet or savory. This version is filled with roasted vegetables and accompanied by a creamy Parmesan sauce. For balance, I serve it with a refreshing and crunchy leafy green salad.

ROASTED VEGETABLE PITHIVIERS
and Parmesan sauce

SERVES 3–4

2 bell peppers

1 pound (400 grams) pumpkin or squash

3 red onions

3 tablespoons olive oil

2–3 green or Chinese cabbage leaves

1 teaspoon dried oregano

3 sprigs of thyme

2 all-butter puff pastry sheets

1 egg yolk

½ cup (100 ml) whipping cream

¼ cup (50 grams) Parmesan cheese

- parchment paper, baking sheet, plastic wrap

PREHEAT the oven to 450°F (220°C). Cut the bell peppers in half and remove the seeds and membrane. Place the bell pepper halves on the baking sheet lined with parchment paper, cut side down. Cut the pumpkin and onions into 2-cm chunks or wedges and place them alongside the bell peppers.

ROAST the vegetables for 20–25 minutes in the preheated oven until the pumpkin or squash and onion are done and the bell pepper is blistered with charred spots.

TAKE the baking sheet out of the oven and cover with a clean kitchen towel. Allow the vegetables to cool to room temperature.

COOK the cabbage leaves for 1 minute in salted water. Remove them from the pan and allow them to drain thoroughly on a second clean kitchen towel.

REMOVE the skin from the pumpkin or squash and the peppers and cut the peppers into strips. Put the roasted pumpkin, red onion, and bell pepper into a bowl along with the thyme leaves and oregano. Add salt and pepper to taste.

LINE a second bowl (with an opening of the same approximate size as the pie dish) with plastic wrap. Now place the cabbage leaves in the bowl so that they overlap. (They should completely enclose the roasted vegetables when they're added.)

SPOON in the vegetable mixture and press down firmly. Fold the cabbage leaves over the vegetables to close. Then wrap the plastic wrap tightly and put the bowl into the refrigerator for at least 4 hours.

PREHEAT the oven to 400°F (200°C). Allow the puff pastry to thaw at room temperature. Roll one sheet of puff pastry into a circle about 7 inches (16 cm) in diameter. This is easy to do if you cut around a small plate or small springform pan. Then roll the second pastry sheet into a larger circle of about 11 inches (28 cm) in diameter (this circle will be trimmed to size later).

TAKE the bowl with the filling out of the refrigerator and fold back the plastic wrap at the top. Invert the filling onto a plate, making sure the filling remains rounded and compact. Remove the rest of the plastic wrap, and pat dry with paper towels.

PLACE the small puff pastry circle onto the baking sheet (on a new sheet of parchment paper). Place the vegetable filling on top of the circle, pressing gently if necessary to keep it round. Lightly brush the pastry around the filling with egg yolk.

COVER the vegetables with the large puff pastry circle and smooth it firmly over the filling. Press the large puff pastry circle onto the small one, and trim neatly with a knife. With a fork, press a pattern into the outside edge.

LIGHTLY brush the pastry with egg yolk and allow to dry for 15 minutes. Cut a small 2-cm circle from the remaining puff pastry with a cutter or a knife. Set aside.

WITH a sharp paring knife, score a fan pattern into the pithivier, starting at the top. Place the small pastry circle you set aside right at the top and poke a small hole in it with a skewer.

BAKE the pithivier in the preheated oven for about 30 minutes until baked through and golden brown.

MEANWHILE heat the whipping cream in a small saucepan. Add the Parmesan cheese and allow to melt. Season with pepper.

TAKE the pithivier out of the oven and allow it to rest for 5 minutes. Cut it into generous slices and serve with the Parmesan sauce.

Preparation time: 45 minutes
Waiting time: 4 hours
Baking time: 50–55 minutes

Beefsteak tomatoes are
firm and their size makes
them ideal for stuffing.

STUFFED BEEFSTEAK TOMATOES
with lime ricotta and herb pesto

**RISOTTO WITH
HONEY-DRIZZLED TOMATOES**
and buffalo ricotta

I often use beefsteak tomatoes cold, but stuffed and baked they form a fantastic centerpiece for a substantial summer salad. My favorite ratio for the herb pesto is 2 parts basil, 1 part dill, and 1 part parsley, but feel free to experiment.

STUFFED BEEFSTEAK TOMATOES
with lime ricotta and herb pesto

SERVES 4

4 beefsteak tomatoes

1 cup (250 grams) ricotta

2 limes

2 handfuls of herbs (basil, dill, and flat-leaf parsley)

½ cup (45 grams) of grated Parmesan cheese

1 tablespoon pine nuts

1 garlic clove

6 tablespoons extra-virgin olive oil

- baking dish, immersion blender

PREHEAT the oven to 400°F (200°C). Slice the tops off of the tomatoes and hollow them out with a spoon. Place the tomatoes in the baking dish.

PUT the ricotta into a bowl. Scrub the limes and grate the green zest into the ricotta. Finely chop half of the herbs and mix into the ricotta along with half of the Parmesan and a little salt and pepper. Fill the tomatoes with the ricotta mixture.

PUT the rest of the herbs and the pine nuts, garlic, and olive oil into a tall measuring or blending cup and blend with the immersion blender until smooth. Stir in the rest of the grated Parmesan and season the pesto with salt and pepper. Spoon a dollop of pesto onto each tomato.

PLACE the tops back onto the tomatoes and roast them in the preheated oven for 10–15 minutes until done but not too soft (this will depend on how juicy they are).

Preparation time: 20 minutes

Baking time: 10-15 minutes

While the cherry tomatoes are turning all sweet and juicy in the oven, you can prepare the risotto on the stove. I always roast the tomatoes in a baking or roasting pan that's large enough to hold the risotto so none of the delicious juices go to waste. To bring out the pure tomato flavor, this risotto is made with water instead of stock, so it's essential to season well with salt and pepper.

RISOTTO WITH HONEY-DRIZZLED TOMATOES
and buffalo ricotta

SERVES 4

3 ¾ cup (750 grams) cherry tomatoes

1 tablespoon liquid honey

4 tablespoons olive oil

2 shallots

1 ½ cup (300 grams) risotto rice

½ cup (150 ml) dry white wine

1 cup (250 grams) buffalo ricotta

¼ cup (50 grams) Parmesan cheese

a handful of basil leaves

- large baking dish

PREHEAT the oven to 400°F (200°C). Cut the cherry tomatoes in half and place them in a large baking dish. Drizzle the tomatoes with the honey and 2 tablespoons olive oil. Sprinkle with salt and pepper.

ROAST the tomatoes in the preheated oven for 25 minutes until they're juicy.

CHOP the shallots finely. For the risotto, heat 2 tablespoons olive oil in a wide heavy-bottomed pan. Fry the shallot for 1 minute.

STIR in the rice and fry until the grains are shiny and translucent. Pour in the wine and allow the rice to absorb the wine as it simmers gently. Add 4 ¼ cups (1 liter) of hot water a third at a time. Allow the rice to absorb each amount of water before adding the next third. Stirring frequently, cook the risotto for about 20 minutes until tender but still firm.

REMOVE the risotto from the heat. Grate the Parmesan. Stir the ricotta and half of the Parmesan cheese into the risotto; the ricotta doesn't need to be fully mixed in.

TAKE the tomatoes out of the oven. Stir the risotto into the tomatoes and all of the roasting juices. Season the risotto well with salt and pepper. Sprinkle with the basil leaves.

SERVE the risotto in the baking dish, with the rest of the Parmesan cheese on the side.

Preparation time: 40 minutes

Romano peppers are ideal for stuffing and grilling on the barbecue. These are filled with marinated feta, but couscous or rice, roasted vegetables and mozzarella, or a mix of spinach, ricotta, and grated Parmesan work well, too. In bad weather, you can grill the peppers in a grill pan or broil them in the oven until soft.

BARBECUED ROMANO PEPPERS
with marinated feta

SERVES 4

4 good-sized red Romano (sweet pointed) peppers

6 ounces (200 grams) feta cheese

1 lemon

12 sprigs of thyme

1 tablespoon olive oil

- kitchen twine

SLIT the side of the peppers and carefully remove the seeds and membrane.

BREAK the feta into chunks. Scrub the lemon and grate off half of the yellow zest. Strip the leaves from 4 thyme sprigs.

STIR the olive oil into the feta along with the lemon zest and thyme leaves. Fill the peppers with the marinated feta.

PRESS them firmly shut and wrap with a piece of kitchen twine. Tuck the remaining thyme sprigs under the twine.

GRIL the peppers on the hot barbecue for 8–10 minutes until the feta is soft and creamy.

Preparation time: 15 minutes
Barbecue time: 10 minutes

The classic "Wellington" beef encased in puff pastry was named after the first Duke of Wellington, who is best known for defeating Napoleon at Waterloo. In this recipe, the pastry is wrapped around butternut squash, which remains tender and very juicy, and the cavity inside the squash is just begging to be filled. The special barrel-aged feta used here has spent a few months ripening in oak barrels, which gives the cheese a more pungent and distinctive flavor. Regular feta is a perfectly acceptable alternative.

BUTTERNUT SQUASH WELLINGTON

with barrel-aged feta

SERVES 4

1 butternut squash
1 garlic clove
1 tablespoon olive oil
2 ounces (50 grams) arugula
3 ½ ounces (100 grams) barrel-aged feta
chili flakes to taste
2 sheets frozen puff pastry
1 egg
- baking sheet with parchment paper

PREHEAT the oven to 350°F (180°C). Cut the butternut squash in half lengthwise. Scoop the strings and seeds out of the cavity with a spoon.

MINCE the garlic. Heat the olive oil in a frying pan. Fry the garlic for 1 minute. Add the arugula and stir-fry until just wilted. Coarsely crumble the feta. Stir the feta into the arugula along with chili flakes to taste.

FILL the cavities of the squash with the arugula-feta mixture and press firmly.

UNROLL the sheets of puff pastry dough on their baking paper. Place a butternut squash half on each sheet of pastry, cut side up. Fold the sides over the squash first, followed by the rest of the dough. Press the seams firmly and trim off any excess dough.

PLACE the pastry-wrapped squash halves on the baking sheet, seam side down. Beat the egg and brush lightly onto the dough.

BAKE the butternut squash Wellingtons in the preheated oven for about 45 minutes until baked through and golden brown. Test the squash for doneness by inserting a metal or wooden skewer. Larger squash will need to bake longer (cover with foil if the pastry starts to get too dark).

Preparation time: 20 minutes
Baking time: 45 minutes

Confit refers to the technique of slow cooking in oil or fat at a low temperature. This recipe uses olive oil, with a seasoning of orange, garlic, and coriander seeds. The delicate flavor and bite of the pumpkin combines beautifully with goat cheese, but also with burrata or buffalo mozzarella. This is a great dish for a special dinner. Pumpkin confit is also lovely served at room temperature as a starter, between courses, or as a main dish with crispy baby potatoes (see page 96) or as a side dish.

SLOW-COOKED PUMPKIN CONFIT
with creamy cheese and crisp basil

SERVES 2–4

½ small organic pumpkin (preferably Hokkaido or similar)

1 ¾ cup (400 ml) olive oil

½ orange

2 garlic cloves

½ teaspoon coriander seeds

10 basil leaves

a handful of arugula or lettuce mix

5 ½ ounces (150 grams) creamy goat or sheep's milk cheese at room temperature

- zester, mortar and pestle

WASH the pumpkin and cut it in half. Scoop out the strings and seeds with a spoon. Slice the pumpkin into wedges 3 inches (7–8 mm) wide. Place them in a small frying pan and pour in enough olive oil to just cover the pumpkin.

SCRUB the orange and use a zester to remove the zest in thin strips. Cut the garlic in half lengthwise. Coarsely grind the coriander seeds in a mortar. Add the strips of orange zest to the olive oil along with the garlic and coriander seeds.

PLACE the pan over medium heat and heat until the olive oil starts to bubble. Turn down the heat to low, cover the pan with a lid, and allow the pumpkin to cook slowly for 10–15 minutes until tender but not falling apart.

REMOVE the pumpkin wedges from the oil with a skimmer or slotted spoon and place them in a serving dish. In the oil the pumpkin was cooked in, fry the basil leaves for a few seconds until crisp. Allow them to drain on paper towels.

SERVE arugula or lettuce mix and the cheese alongside the pumpkin. Spoon on a little of the olive oil from the pan. Sprinkle with the crispy basil leaves and pepper to taste.

Preparation time: 30 minutes

This is the perfect dish for a dinner party. The pumpkin can be served lukewarm as a starter, as a first course, or as a main dish.

I first tried beurre noisette mayonnaise at a restaurant in Amsterdam: a wonderful creation in which the oil in the mayonnaise is replaced with beurre noisette, or "hazelnut butter" which is butter that's melted and cooked over a low heat until it takes on the aroma, color, and flavor of hazelnuts. Store the mayonnaise in a cool place, but not in the refrigerator.

HASSELBACK BUTTERNUT SQUASH
with beurre noisette mayonnaise

SERVES 4

1 cup (250 grams) unsalted butter

2 small butternut squash

2 teaspoons ground cumin

1 bunch of thyme

6 tablespoons extra-virgin olive oil

2 teaspoons coarse sea salt

1 egg

1 teaspoon mustard

3 tablespoons white wine vinegar

2 ounces (50 grams) baby leaf lettuce

2 teaspoons capers

- baking sheet with parchment paper, immersion blender

START up to a day in advance by making the beurre noisette. Cut the butter into pieces. Place them in a saucepan with a light-colored bottom (to see the color of the butter). Allow to melt over low heat. The butter will start to foam, and the fat, proteins, and water will separate out. Allow the butter to brown slowly.

TAKE the pan off of the heat when the butter is not quite hazelnut brown, because it will continue to darken somewhat. Pour the beurre noisette into a small bowl and allow to cool.

PREHEAT the oven to 450°F (220°C). Peel the squash with a peeler and then cut both butternut squash in half lengthwise. Scoop the seeds and strings out of the cavities. Place the halves on the baking sheet, cut side down.

CUT the squash into thin slices, but don't go all the way through, so that the halves stay intact! Sprinkle the cumin into the slits and tuck in some thyme sprigs here and there.

DRIZZLE the squash with 4 tablespoons olive oil and sprinkle with the sea salt. Roast in the oven for 30 minutes until done.

PLACE the egg into a tall measuring cup along with the mustard and 1 tablespoon wine vinegar. Slowly pour in the beurre noisette. Blend with the immersion blender into a thick, creamy mayonnaise.

MAKE a dressing with the remaining 2 tablespoons olive oil and 2 tablespoons wine vinegar and toss with the lettuce. Sprinkle on the capers and some pepper. Serve the squash with the salad and the beurre noisette mayonnaise.

Preparation time: 30 minutes

Baking time: 30 minute

The origins of this dish can be traced back to the former province of Dauphiné in southern France. Usually made with new potatoes only, in this recipe we replace half of them with sweet potatoes and parboil the potato slices to halve the oven time. Make the salsa when the gratin comes out of the oven so the arugula remains fresh and crunchy. Allowing the gratin to rest for a few minutes will make it firmer and easier to cut into neat slices.

GRATIN DAUPHINOIS
with sweet potato and arugula-ginger salsa

SERVES 4

1 pound (400 grams) baby potatoes

1 pound (400 grams) sweet potatoes

1 ¼ cups (300 ml) whole milk

1 cup (200 ml) whipping cream

1 garlic clove

3 sprigs of rosemary

2 cups (150 grams) grated Gruyère

2 ounces (25 grams) arugula

a ½-inch (1-cm) piece of fresh ginger

2 teaspoons capers

3 tablespoons extra-virgin olive oil

1 teaspoon ginger syrup or honey

- mandoline (optional), baking dish 9 inch (24 cm)

PREHEAT the oven to 400°F (200°C). Scrub the potatoes; peeling isn't necessary, but you can if you like. Slice the potatoes on the mandoline or cut them with a sharp knife into slices ¾ inch (1–2 mm) thick.

PLACE the potato slices into a pan along with the milk and whipping cream. Then cut the garlic into thin slices and add them to the pan along with the rosemary. Cook the potatoes for 5 minutes.

WITH a skimmer or slotted spoon, transfer a layer of potatoes to the baking dish. For every layer, sprinkle on some of the cheese and salt and pepper, making sure that the last layer is just potatoes.

REDUCE the milk-cream mixture until it has thickened into a sauce, then pour it over the potato slices in the baking dish. Bake the potato gratin in the preheated oven for 20–25 minutes until golden brown.

REMOVE the gratin from the oven and allow it to rest while you make the salsa. Coarsely chop the arugula or leave it whole. Peel and grate the ginger. Coarsely chop the capers.

MIX the ginger with the capers, olive oil, and ginger syrup or honey, then mix in the arugula.

ARRANGE the arugula salsa on top of the gratin and serve at once.

Preparation time: 30 minutes
Baking time: 20-25 minutes

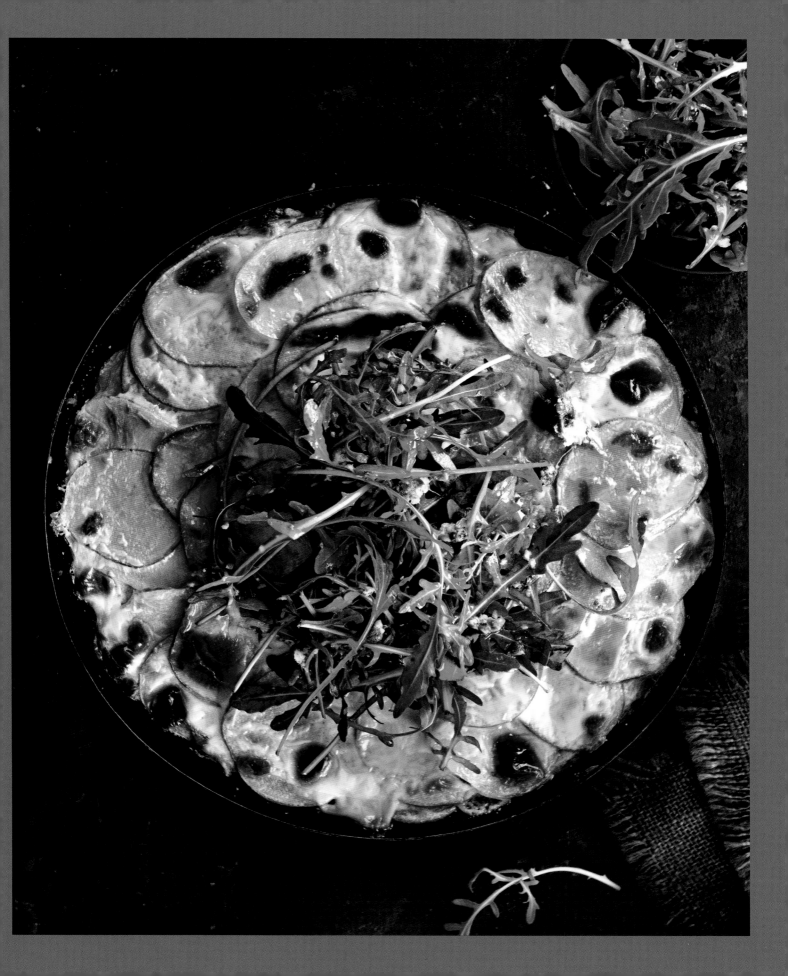

Prepare the topping while the sweet corn is roasting in the oven. Olive herb both smells and tastes of olives. If you can't find it, you can replace it with finely minced black olives and a sprinkling of fresh thyme or oregano.

ROASTED SWEET CORN
with garlicky yogurt and olive herb

SERVES 4

4 ears of sweet corn, husked and ready to cook

2 tablespoons olive oil

½ cup (100 grams) Greek yogurt

1 garlic clove

1 teaspoon (black) sesame seeds

3 ounces (75 grams) soft goat cheese or feta

2 tablespoons olive herb

smoked paprika

- shallow baking dish

PREHEAT the oven to 450°F (220°C). Place the ears of corn in the baking dish. Drizzle them with the olive oil and sprinkle with a little salt.

ROAST the corn in the preheated oven for about 30 minutes until cooked and golden brown.

MIX the Greek yogurt with the grated or pressed garlic clove. Toast the sesame seeds in a dry frying pan. Crumble the goat cheese or feta.

PLACE the roasted ears of corn in a serving dish and top with the garlicky yogurt, cheese crumbles, and olive herb. Sprinkle on some smoked paprika and the sesame seeds.

Preparation time: 15 minutes

Baking time: 30 minutes

Artichokes need to be cooked for about thirty minutes, which can be done ahead of time. Likewise, the olive crumbs and olive mayonnaise can be prepared in advance. These artichokes can be served as a starter, and they also make a lovely entrée along with a salad and either bread or pan-fried baby potatoes.

CRUNCHY ARTICHOKES
with olive mayonnaise

SERVES 4

2 artichokes
juice of 1 lemon
2 slices white sandwich bread
1 teaspoon olive oil
¾ cup (150 grams) olives with garlic
3 ½ tablespoons (50 grams) mayonnaise
1 sprig of parsley
- immersion blender with chopper attachment, baking sheet

CUT the artichokes in half lengthwise. Remove the fuzzy choke and the innermost leaves. Cook the artichoke halves in water with the lemon juice for about 30 minutes—the artichoke is done when you can easily pull off a leaf.

CHOP the bread slices (with crust) in the chopper into fine breadcrumbs, along with the olive oil and ¼ cup (50 grams) of the olives. Add salt to taste.

BLEND the remaining ½ cup (100 grams) olives with the mayonnaise and 1 tablespoon water in the immersion blender until thick and creamy.

PREHEAT the oven to 400°F (200°C). Allow the artichokes to drain well. Place them on the baking sheet, cut side up, and top with the olive breadcrumbs.

BAKE the artichokes for 15–20 minutes, until the breadcrumbs are golden brown and crunchy. Finely chop the parsley.

SERVE the artichoke halves on 4 plates, sprinkle with the parsley, and dollops of olive mayonnaise.

Preparation time: 45 minutes
Baking time: 15–20 minutes

When I used to make cannelloni, I would struggle because the rolls usually didn't fit neatly into the baking pan. The whole process has become a lot more relaxed since I've started cutting the cannelloni into pieces and putting them into the dish haphazardly. If you're making the mini-cannelloni for a special dinner, you can do a lot of the prep in advance. You can prepare the filling the day before and roll the lasagna sheets around it. Cover, and store the rolls in the refrigerator.

MINI-CANNELLONI
with roasted sweet potatoes and buffalo mozzarella

SERVES 4

6 cups (800 grams) sweet potatoes

4 tablespoons olive oil

1 cup (250 grams) ricotta

a handful of grated Parmesan cheese

8 sprigs of thyme leaves

2 garlic cloves

2 ½ cups (500 grams) cherry tomatoes

12 fresh lasagna sheets

½ cup (50 grams) butter

⅓ cup (60 grams) flour

½ cup (150 ml) dry white wine

2 ¼ cups (500 ml) milk

1 ball of buffalo mozzarella (4 ½ ounces/125 grams)

- baking sheet with parchment paper, shallow baking dish

PREHEAT the oven to 450°F (220°C). Peel the sweet potatoes and cut them into 1-inch (2-cm) pieces. Distribute the sweet potato pieces over the baking sheet and drizzle with 2 tablespoons olive oil.

ROAST the sweet potato in the oven for 15–20 until done and completely soft. Allow to cool to room temperature.

MASH the sweet potato well, then mix with the ricotta, Parmesan cheese, thyme leaves from 5 of the springs, and salt and pepper.

LOWER the oven temperature to 350°F (180°C). Mince the garlic.

HEAT 2 tablespoons olive oil in a frying pan. Fry the garlic for 1 minute. Stir in the cherry tomatoes and cook gently until the juices are released. Transfer the tomatoes and the pan juices to the baking dish.

DIVIDE the sweet potato-ricotta filling over the lasagna sheets and roll them up. Cut each roll into 3 pieces and place the mini-cannelloni on the tomatoes.

MELT the butter in a frying pan. Add the flour and cook for 1 minute. Slowly whisk in the wine. Then add the milk and whisk until the sauce is smooth. Allow the sauce to cook gently for 5 minutes.

POUR the béchamel sauce over the pasta rolls. Tear the mozzarella into pieces and arrange them on top of the sauce, then add salt and pepper and the leaves from the 3 remaining springs of thyme.

BAKE the cannelloni for 30 minutes until cooked through and golden brown.

Preparation time: 40 minutes

Baking time: 45-50 minutes

CAPUNSEI WITH BABY ASPARAGUS

and lemon gremolata

plant not only look elegant, but their appearance is enhanced by their delicate flavor and crunchy bite. They're also available as asparagus tips, in both green and white.

LEMON These beauties are tiger lemons. While the tiger is the king of the jungle, the lemon does a lot of heavy lifting in the kitchen. Like a pinch of salt, a splash of lemon juice can really lift the flavor of a dish. You can add it either during preparation or afterwards. Lime and yuzu, a Japanese citrus fruit, are great flavor boosters too.

ARROZ MELOSO
with dry-cured olives and
green asparagus

Every other day, I bake a sourdough loaf. As soon as the fresh bread comes out of the oven, my family loses interest in the "old" bread. Luckily, there are plenty of recipes for stale bread. In the Italian city of Mantova, people add stock, egg, and a handful of grated Parmesan to make a delicious version of gnocchi called capunsei.

CAPUNSEI WITH BABY ASPARAGUS
and lemon gremolata

SERVES 4

16 ounces (450 grams) stale
bread

¾ cup (400 ml) hot
vegetable stock

2 eggs

¼ cup of grated Parmesan
cheese

flour

1 lemon

1 garlic clove

1 sprig of parsley

6 tablespoons extra-virgin
olive oil

1 pound (400 grams) baby
green asparagus

- food processor or
immersion blender with
chopper attachment,
plastic wrap

CHOP the bread into fine breadcrumbs in the food processor or in small batches in the chopper. Transfer the breadcrumbs to a bowl and pour in the heated stock. Cover and allow to stand for 2 hours.

MIX the eggs and the Parmesan into the soaked breadcrumbs. Shape this mixture into a ball, cover with plastic wrap, and refrigerate for 2 hours.

SHAPE the mixture into small balls and roll them between your hands into long tapered dumplings. If the dough is sticky, add a little flour. Set aside the bread "gnocchi" on a platter or wooden cutting board dusted with flour until ready to cook.

ZEST the lemon. Grate or press the garlic. Finely chop the parsley. Mix the lemon zest with the garlic and parsley (= gremolata).

HEAT 2 tablespoons olive oil in a frying pan. Fry the asparagus for 4 minutes until just tender. Cook the bread "gnocchi" in plenty of salted water for 3–4 minutes; they are done when they rise to the surface. Scoop them out with a skimmer or slotted spoon and add them to the asparagus.

MIX the gremolata with 4 tablespoons olive oil. Spoon the bread "gnocchi" and asparagus onto 4 plates. Top with the gremolata and sprinkle with salt and pepper to taste. Serve with a little extra grated Parmesan cheese.

Preparation time: 30 minutes

Waiting time: 4 hours

Cooking time: 15 minutes

South of the Spanish city of Valencia, in the region of Albufera, you will find vast rice fields. This is where the short, round grain that's used in paella is cultivated. Few outside Spain are aware that this rice is used in other dishes too. Whereas the rice in paella is cooked until all the liquid has been absorbed, arroz meloso remains a little runny. It's similar to risotto, but without the addition of dairy, so the flavor is very pure and unadulterated.

ARROZ MELOSO
with dry-cured olives and green asparagus

SERVES 4

2 garlic cloves

5 tablespoons olive oil

2 teaspoons smoked paprika

1 ½ cups (300 grams) paella rice

1 cup (150 ml) dry white wine

1 liter vegetable stock

1 ½ pounds (700 grams) green asparagus

1 lemon

2 sprigs of parsley

¾ cup (150 grams) (dry-cured) black olives

MINCE the garlic. Heat 3 tablespoons olive oil in a wide heavy-bottomed pan. Fry the garlic and the smoked paprika for 1 minute.

STIR in the rice and fry until the grains are shiny and translucent. Pour in the wine and allow the rice to absorb the wine as it simmers gently. Add the stock a third at a time; allow the rice to simmer gently and absorb each amount of stock before adding the next third. Stirring frequently, cook the rice for about 20 minutes until tender but still firm.

CUT off the woody ends of the asparagus spears. Cut them into pieces 1 ¼ inches (3–4 cm) long.

HEAT the remaining 2 tablespoons olive oil in a frying pan. Fry the asparagus pieces for 5 minutes until just tender. Scrub the lemon and grate off the yellow zest. Finely chop the parsley. Stir the lemon zest and the parsley into the asparagus and fry a bit longer.

REMOVE the rice from the heat while it's still fluid. Stir the olives and the fried asparagus into the rice. Season the arroz meloso with salt and pepper.

Preparation time: 30 minutes

Warm Camembert, soft and creamy inside and crusty on top is as good as it sounds! It's best to use an ovenproof dish that can go straight on the table, because the warm cheese will be too soft to transfer onto another plate. Great with roasted vegetables or slices of French bread and a salad.

WARM CAMEMBERT
with lemon and thyme

SERVES 4

1 Camembert (9 ounces/
250 grams)
1 slice white sandwich bread
1 lemon
3 sprigs of thyme
2 teaspoons olive oil
- shallow baking dish,
immersion blender with
chopper attachment

PREHEAT the oven to 400°F (200°C). Remove the Camembert from its wrapping and place the cheese in a small baking dish.

PLACE the bread (with crust) in the chopper of the immersion blender and process into fine breadcrumbs. Sprinkle the breadcrumbs into a deep plate.

ZEST the lemon. Strip the leaves from the thyme sprigs. Mix the lemon zest into the breadcrumbs along with the thyme, olive oil, and pepper to taste.

DISTRIBUTE the breadcrumbs over the Camembert. Bake in the preheated oven for about 10 minutes, until the breadcrumbs are golden brown.

Preparation time: 10 minutes
Baking time: 10 minutes

Warm Camembert
is soft and creamy
inside with a crispy
crust. It really is as
good as it sounds!

ROTOLO
with roasted green asparagus

Don't let the length of this recipe put you off: it's time-consuming, but worth every step. This rotolo brings something exceptional to the table, even though the flavors are familiar. You can swap the roasted asparagus for other roasted or grilled vegetables. For a special dinner, I usually prepare the pasta roll in advance and keep it in the refrigerator, wrapped in plastic wrap. For extra festive occasions, I bake and serve rotolos in pretty individual oven dishes.

ROTOLO
with roasted green asparagus

SERVES 4

¾ cup (100 grams) flour

¾ cup (100 grams) semolina

2 eggs

4 tablespoons olive oil

1 ¼ pounds (500 grams) green asparagus

1 cup (250 grams) ricotta

1 lemon

1 ½ cups (75 grams) semi-dried (cherry) tomatoes

1 garlic clove

2 ¼ cup (500 ml) passata (sieved tomatoes)

1 ball of mozzarella (4 ½ ounces/125 grams)

a handful of coarsely chopped arugula, and/or basil

extra-virgin olive oil

- food processor or mixer with dough hooks, plastic wrap, baking sheet with parchment paper, clean kitchen towel, kitchen twine, baking dish 9 inch (24 cm)

KNEAD (with the food processor or mixer) the two flours, the eggs, 1 tablespoon olive oil, and a pinch of salt into a smooth and elastic dough. Wrap the dough in plastic wrap and allow it to rest in the refrigerator for at least 30 minutes.

PREHEAT the oven to 450°F (220°C). Cut off the woody ends of the asparagus. Cut thick spears in half lengthwise. Arrange the asparagus on the baking sheet and drizzle with 2 tablespoon olive oil. Roast the asparagus in the oven for 20 minutes until just tender. Take them out of the oven and allow to cool.

LIGHTLY dust a work surface with flour. Roll out the pasta dough into a rectangle 1 mm thick. Trim the piece of dough to about 11 x 14 inch (36 x 30 cm) and place in on the kitchen towel.

SPREAD the ricotta over the dough. Scrub the lemon and grate the yellow zest over the ricotta. Add the asparagus spears, placing them lengthwise onto the ricotta so they will roll easily along with the dough. Cut the semi-dried tomatoes into pieces and distribute them over the asparagus. Sprinkle with a little salt and pepper.

ROLL the dough up fairly tightly (starting at the long side of the dough and roll. Now tightly wrap the pasta roll in a kitchen towel and tie the ends shut with a piece of kitchen twine. In a large fish poacher or other pan, bring plenty of salted water to a boil. Place the roll in the cooking water, towel and all, and simmer gently for 30–35 minutes until done. Make sure the roll stays submerged.

PREHEAT the oven to 450°F (220°C). Take the pasta roll out of the pan and allow it to rest, still wrapped in the towel, for 5 minutes. Mince the garlic. Heat the passata with the garlic and 1 tablespoon olive oil. Pour this tomato sauce into the baking dish.

REMOVE the towel and cut the pasta roll into 1½-cm slices. Place them in the tomato sauce. Tear the mozzarella into pieces and distribute the pieces over the pasta.

BAKE the pasta for about 10 minutes, until the cheese has melted and starts to brown. Remove from the oven and sprinkle with the herbs and drizzle with extra-virgin olive oil.

Preparation time: 1 hour
Waiting time: 30 minutes
Baking time: 30 minutes

This is by far the easiest—and tastiest—way of preparing asparagus: just slide them into the oven and let the heat work its magic and intensify their flavor. I like to serve them the traditional way with melted butter and a poached egg. The prospect of poaching an egg might put some people off, but this is a fail-safe method! Serve with skin-on boiled or steamed baby potatoes.

ROASTED WHITE ASPARAGUS
with poached egg and parsley butter

SERVES 4

4 ½ pounds (2 kilos) white asparagus

4 tablespoons olive oil

½ cup (125 grams) unsalted butter

2 sprigs of parsley

3 tablespoons vinegar

4 eggs

- baking sheet with parchment paper

PREHEAT the oven to 350°F (180°C). Cut the woody ends off the asparagus, peel the asparagus and then place them on the baking sheet.

DRIZZLE the asparagus with the olive oil and a little salt. Roast the asparagus in the preheated oven for about 30 minutes until just tender. The exact baking time depends on the thickness of the asparagus and the desired degree of doneness: test for doneness by piercing the asparagus with the tip of a sharp knife.

MELT the butter in a saucepan over low heat. Finely chop the parsley.

IN a sauté pan, bring a generous layer of water to a boil along with the vinegar. Turn down the heat to low so that the water is no longer at a rolling boil—the water should just simmer gently!

BREAK 1 egg into a coffee cup. Slip the egg slowly into the water. Repeat with the other 3 eggs. Make sure the eggs don't touch each other; you can also poach the eggs 2 at a time.

POACH the eggs for 3–4 minutes until the egg white is cooked and the yolk is to your liking, either very soft or nearly hard. Lift the eggs out of the water with a skimmer or slotted spoon, allow to drain briefly, then put on a plate.

DIVIDE the roasted asparagus over 4 plates, then add a poached egg to each plate. Stir the parsley and salt to taste into the melted butter. Pour the parsley butter over the egg and asparagus on each plate. Sprinkle with pepper and serve at once.

Preparation time: 30 minutes
Baking time: 30 minutes

"Al cartoccio" is the Italian equivalent of the French "en papillote." Literally "in parchment," in this method food is cooked wrapped in aluminum foil or parchment paper. These tasty pasta parcels bring a surprise to the table and are lots of fun at a dinner party. Even better, you can prepare the parcels in advance and keep them in the refrigerator! Make sure to add an extra 4 to 5 minutes to the baking time if you put the parcels into the oven straight from the fridge. Once in the oven, the cheese melts and all of the flavors mingle.

PASTA AL CARTOCCIO
with braised fennel and Stilton

SERVES 4

⅔ pound (300 grams) tagliatelle or spaghetti

2 shallots

1 ¼ pounds (500 grams) fennel

3 tablespoons olive oil

1 cup (150 ml) dry white wine

1 jar (5 ounce/150 grams) semi-sun-dried tomatoes in oil

6 ounces (200 grams) Stilton cheese

- immersion blender, 4 sheets of parchment paper, kitchen twine, baking sheet

COOK the tagliatelle or spaghetti al dente according to the packet instructions. Finely chop the shallot and cut the fennel into thin strips. Reserve the fennel greens.

HEAT the olive oil in a Dutch oven or heavy-bottomed pan. Fry the shallot for 1 minute. Stir in the fennel and fry for 3 minutes, but don't allow it to brown.

POUR in the wine and bring to a boil. Turn down the heat to low, cover, and braise the fennel for 10 minutes.

PREHEAT the oven to 350°F (180°C). With the immersion blender, purée the tomatoes and 1–2 tablespoons of the oil from the jar until smooth.

DRAIN the pasta, then mix with the puréed tomatoes. Spoon the pasta onto the sheets of parchment paper, and top with the fennel and Stilton. Sprinkle with the reserved fennel greens and pepper to taste.

GATHER the parchment paper into pouches and tie them shut with pieces of kitchen twine. Put them on the baking sheet.

BAKE the pasta pouches in the preheated oven for 10 minutes, until the cheese has melted.

TRANSFER the pouches to 4 plates and let everyone open theirs at the table.

Preparation time: 25 minutes
Baking time: 10 minutes

This chili oil is great when, like me, you would like a bit of extra heat. You can use it on just about anything. I use sunflower oil as a base for Asian dishes and olive oil for Mediterranean food. Warming the oil releases the aroma of the chilies. Only add the garlic after you've taken the pan off the heat to prevent it from burning and imparting a bitter flavor. If the chili oil is too fiery for your liking, you can add some more oil.

CHILI OIL
with garlic

BASIC RECIPE

1 ¼ cups (150 ml) sunflower or olive oil

1 tablespoon dried chili flakes

2 garlic cloves

- small clean bottle

GENTLY heat the oil and the chili flakes in a saucepan.

REMOVE the pan from the heat. Grate the garlic into the chili oil and allow to cool to room temperature.

POUR the chili oil into the bottle and store in the refrigerator. Use within four days.

Preparation time: 10 minutes + cooling time

A giant lumpia, or egg roll, the kind that's crispy, full of fresh vegetables, and almost too big for my plate is one of my top three snacks. Feel free to use other ingredients such as mushrooms, carrots, zucchini, or bell peppers. Serve the lumpia with sweet chili sauce or soy sauce and the chili oil on the previous page to give the vegetables a bit of a kick.

GIANT LEEK LUMPIA
with bean sprouts, omelet, and edamame

SERVES 4

20 egg roll (lumpia) wrappers
1 ¼ pounds (800 grams) leeks
4 tablespoons sunflower oil
4 eggs
½ cup (100 grams) bean sprouts
¾ cup (100 grams) edamame
oil for deep-frying
sweet chili sauce and/or soy sauce with chili oil to serve

THAW the egg roll wrappers underneath a damp kitchen towel.

SLICE the leeks into rings. Heat 2 tablespoons oil in a wok, then stir-fry the leeks for 5–6 minutes until soft.

BEAT the eggs with salt and pepper. Heat the remaining 2 tablespoons oil in a frying pan. Pour the egg mixture into the pan and fry the omelet for 2–3 minutes on each side until cooked through and golden brown.

BRUSH the edges of 4 egg roll wrappers with water and place them on a clean kitchen towel to form a large square measuring 14 x 14 inches (35 x 35 cm) allowing the edges of the wrappers to overlap each other slightly. Place this large wrapper so that one corner is pointing towards you.

SPOON in a row of ¼ of the leeks, bean sprouts, and edamame in the middle of the wrapper. Cut the omelet into pieces and top the vegetables with ¼ of the omelet.

BRUSH the edges of this large wrapper with water. Fold first the side corners and then the bottom corner over the filling and roll up tightly into a large lumpia. To make the lumpia sturdier, now take an extra wrapper, moisten the edges, and wrap this around the finished lumpia. Make 3 more lumpias in the same way. You can now freeze the lumpias or deep-fry them at once.

HEAT the oil to 350°F (180°C). Deep-fry the lumpias in 2 batches for about 8 minutes until crisp and golden brown. Serve them with a dish of sweet chili sauce and/or soy sauce with chili oil.

Preparation time: 45 minutes

Like onions, leeks can be used in just about everything but are rarely given a starring role. This casserole really captures their sweet and delicate flavor and gives the leek its long-awaited moment in the limelight. Comté has a similarly mild and almost sweet, nutty flavor. This popular cheese originates in eastern France and is made from raw milk. Serve the leeks with pan-fried or roast potatoes.

CREAMY LEEKS
with mustard and Comté

SERVES 4

2 ¼ pounds (1 kilo) leeks

¼ cup (25 grams) butter

½ cup (100 ml) dry white wine

⅔ cup (200 grams) crème fraiche

1 tablespoon mild coarse-ground mustard

1 garlic clove

3 ½ ounces (100 grams) Comté cheese

1 sprig of parsley

- ovenproof frying pan or baking dish

CLEAN the leeks and cut them into pieces 3-4 inches (8–10 cm) long.

MELT the butter in an ovenproof frying pan and fry the leeks for 4 minutes. Pour in ¼ cup wine, cover the pan, and braise the leeks for 10–12 minutes until just tender.

MEANWHILE preheat the oven to 400°F (200°C). Put the crème fraiche in a bowl along with the mustard and the remaining ¼ cup wine. Grate or press in the garlic.

GRATE the cheese. Add to the crème fraiche mixture along with pepper to taste and stir until smooth.

REMOVE the pan from the heat. Transfer the leeks to a baking dish if using. Pour the crème fraiche mixture over the leeks.

BAKE the leeks for 20 minutes until done and golden brown. Finely chop the parsley and sprinkle onto the leeks.

Preparation time: 20 minutes
Baking time: 20 minutes

Onions are often cast in a supporting role. But in this dish, they're the star ingredient: cooked with dark abbey beer, Dutch spice cake or gingerbread, and molasses until they're soft and sweet. Great with the crispy baby potatoes from page 96 or used as a filling for the Parmentier on the next page.

ONION STEW

with abbey beer, apple syrup, and fennel seeds

SERVES 4

6 onions

¼ cup (25 grams) butter

2 slices of Dutch spice cake or gingerbread

1 bottle dark abbey beer or other dark beer

1 tablespoon apple syrup (or molasses)

2 bay leaves

1 teaspoon fennel seeds

PEEL the onions, then cut them in half through the stem end so that the halves remain intact.

MELT the butter in a Dutch oven or heavy-bottomed pan. Place the onions in the pan, cut side down, and fry them for 3 minutes until golden brown. Meanwhile, cut the Dutch spice cake or gingerbread into small cubes.

TURN the onions. Pour the beer down the inside edge of the pan. Add the gingerbread cake along with the molasses, bay leaves, and fennel seeds. Bring to a boil.

TURN down the heat to low, cover the pan, and stew the onions for 10–15 minutes until tender. Season the onion stew with salt and pepper.

Preparation time: 15 minutes

Stewing time: 10-15 minutes

The stewed onions on the previous page are a great base for this vegetarian take on "shepherd's pie," a classic casserole topped with mashed potatoes. The ribbed pattern on the potatoes not only looks pretty, it makes for an extra-crispy crust.

STEWED ONIONS SHEPHERD'S PIE
with rosemary

SERVES 4

2 pounds (1 kilo) russet
potatoes
1 ⅓ pounds (600 grams)
parsnips
1 cup (200 ml) milk
¼ cup (25 grams) butter
2 sprigs of rosemary
1 recipe onion stew
from page 237
- baking dish 8 x 11 inch
(20 x 38 cm)

PEEL the potatoes and parsnips and cut them into pieces 1 ½–2 inches (3–4 cm) long. Cook the potatoes with the parsnips in plenty of salted water for 15-20 minutes until done.

HEAT the milk along with the butter and the rosemary sprigs. Remove the milk from the heat, cover, and allow to infuse for 15 minutes. Meanwhile, heat the onion stew over low heat. Preheat the oven to 400°F (200°C).

TAKE the rosemary sprigs out of the milk. Drain the potatoes and parsnips, and mash them with the rosemary milk until creamy. Add salt and pepper to taste.

TRANSFER the hot onion stew to the baking dish, reserving half of the sauce to serve on the side. Distribute the potato-parsnip mash over the stew and smooth into an even layer. Make attractive ridges in the mash with a fork: keep dipping the fork in a glass of water, as you would with an ice cream scoop.

BAK the shepherd's pie in the preheated oven for about 30 minutes, until crisp and golden brown. Meanwhile, heat the reserved sauce and serve with the shepherd's pie.

Preparation time: 30 minutes
Baking time: 30 minutes

CREAMY PARSNIP GRATIN
with oregano

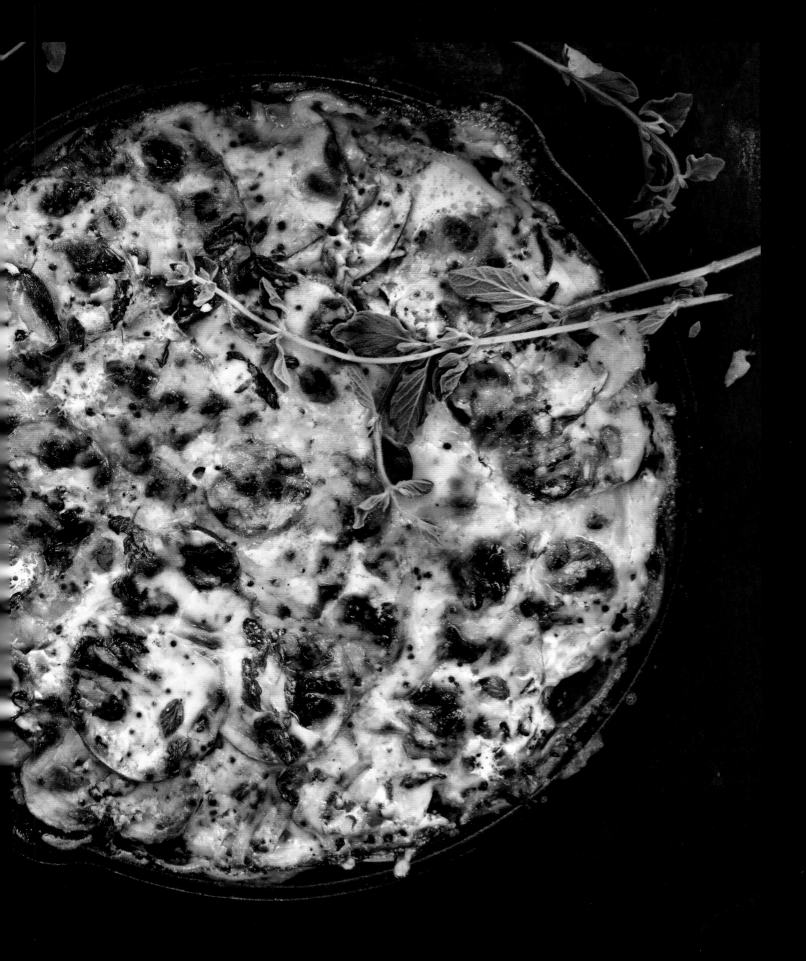

PEPPERCORNS Green peppercorns grow on the pepper plant and are picked while still unripe. Unlike most other peppercorns, they're not dried, and this gives them a more delicate flavor and texture. Green peppercorns are usually preserved in brine and only rarely available fresh. They are delicious in soups and dressings, and especially in a classic pepper sauce.

PAN-FRIED CELERY ROOT
with creamy pepper sauce

This recipe is going to give you a lot of joy. See it as a basic recipe for an extra creamy gratin. I'm using parsnip here, but any combination of vegetables will work. Think squash and pumpkin, potatoes and sweet potatoes, celery root, Jerusalem artichokes, beets, and zucchini. Great with bread and a fresh green leafy salad.

CREAMY PARSNIP GRATIN
with oregano

SERVES 4

1 cup (200 ml) whipping cream
¼ cup (50 ml) milk
1 garlic clove
1 ½ pounds (750 grams) parsnips
6 ounces (200 grams) Swiss cheese (Emmentaler) or Gruyère
⅔ cup (200 grams) crème fraiche
2 tablespoon mild mustard
4–5 sprigs of oregano
- baking dish 9 x 10 inch (22–24 cm)

PREHEAT the oven to 350°F (180°C). Put the whipping cream and milk into a saucepan, grate or press in the garlic clove, and heat over low heat. Do not allow to boil!

SCRUB or peel the parsnips. Shave or cut the parsnips into thin slices ⅛ inch (2–3 mm) thick. Grate the cheese.

REMOVE the cream mixture from the heat and whisk in the crème fraiche, mustard, and the leaves from 3 oregano sprigs.

ARRANGE a third of the parsnips in the baking dish. Sprinkle with a third of the cheese and a little salt and pepper. Pour over one fourth of the cream mixture. Make 2 more layers in the same way. Sprinkle the top layer of cheese with the leaves from 2 oregano sprigs. Pour over the rest of the cream mixture.

BAKE the gratin in the preheated oven for about 30 minutes until cooked through and golden brown.

Preparation time: 20 minutes
Baking time: 30 minutes

A celery root never languishes in my vegetable drawer. I add the root with its velvety aroma to anything from soups and pasta sauces to salads. Or I'll slice it into thin slivers to use in a gratin or mash it into a buttery purée with a generous grating of nutmeg. This one is my favorite: thick slices of celery root pan-fried in butter with a creamy pepper sauce. Served with french fries, a salad, and, of course, homemade mayonnaise.

PAN-FRIED CELERY ROOT

with creamy pepper sauce

SERVES 2

1 small celery root
¼ cup (25 grams) butter
1 tablespoon olive oil
1 shallot
1 tablespoon green pepper-corns (fresh or from a jar)
3 tablespoons Madeira or cognac
½ cup (125 ml) whipping cream
1 sprig of parsley

CUT 4 uniform slices ½ inch (1 cm) thick from the celery root, then peel the slices.

HEAT the butter with the olive oil in 2 large frying pans. Fry the slices for about 15 minutes until cooked through and golden brown on both sides.

PLACE the celery slices in one of the frying pans and cover with a lid to keep them warm.

CHOP the shallot finely. In the cooking fat in the second frying pan, fry the shallot with the peppercorns for 1 minute. Add the Madeira or cognac.

POUR in the whipping cream and allow the sauce to reduce to the desired thickness. Finely chop the parsley.

PLACE the celery root slices onto 2 plates. Spoon on some of the peppercorn cream sauce and sprinkle with the parsley. Serve the rest of the sauce on the side.

Preparation time: 25 minutes

Magor is not one, but two cheeses. This Italian cheese blend consists of layers of mascarpone and Gorgonzola, hence the name. Sometimes sold as gormas, the combination provides both creaminess and piquancy. If you can't find it, you can use 3 ounces (80 grams) of Gorgonzola and 4 ounces (120 grams) of mascarpone instead. In summer, I like to replace the Jerusalem artichokes (sunchokes) with small artichokes.

JERUSALEM ARTICHOKE GRATIN
with magor and Parmesan

SERVES 4

1 ½ pounds (750 grams) Jerusalem artichokes (sunchokes)

1 tablespoon olive oil

½ pound (300 grams) spinach or kale

1 ½ cup (300 ml) whipping cream

1 garlic clove

¼ cup of grated Parmesan cheese

7 ounces (200 grams) magor (or Gorgonzola and mascarpone)

- baking dish

SCRUB the Jerusalem artichokes and cut them in half lengthwise. Cook them for 10–15 minutes until done.

MEANWHILE preheat the oven to 450°F (220°C). Heat the olive oil in a frying pan. Add the spinach or kale and stir-fry until the leaves are wilted; if using kale, add a splash of water or white wine if necessary.

POUR the whipping cream into a measuring cup. Press or grate in the garlic. Stir the Parmesan cheese into the cream, and season with salt and pepper.

DRAIN the Jerusalem artichokes. Arrange them in the baking dish along with the spinach or kale. Tuck pieces of the magor in between (or, if using, tuck in pieces of Gorgonzola and small spoonfuls of mascarpone). Pour over the Parmesan-cream mixture.

BAKE the gratin in the preheated oven for 30 minutes until golden brown.

Preparation time: 30 minutes
Baking time: 30 minutes

I make this easy casserole all year round, using scorzonera in winter, Belgian endive in the fall, and asparagus in spring. Scorzonera is also known as black salsify or black oyster plant, because its flavor is reminiscent of oyster. It can sometimes be difficult to find in markets, so feel free to substitute it with asparagus or endive. I peel the roots under water, so they keep their creamy white color.

SCORZONERA CASSEROLE
with mashed potatoes and herbed crème fraiche

SERVES 4

2 ¼ pounds (1 kilo) starchy potatoes

3 pounds (1 ½ kilos) scorzonera (black salsify), endive, or asparagus

1 garlic clove

3 sprigs of parsley

⅔ cups (200 grams) crème fraiche

1 ¼ cups (100 grams) grated mature Gouda cheese

½ cup (125–150 ml) milk

¼ cup (25 grams) butter

- baking dish 8 x 11 inch (20 x 30 cm), masher or potato ricer

PEEL the potatoes and cut them into pieces. Cook the potatoes for 20 minutes until done. Peel the scorzonera, asparagus, or endive as well, and cook them for 15 minutes until done.

PREHEAT the oven to 400°F (200°C). Grate or press the garlic. Finely chop the parsley. Mix the crème fraiche with the cheese, garlic, and parsley, and season with salt and pepper.

HEAT the milk with the butter. Drain the potatoes. Mash them until smooth or put them through a potato ricer. Stir in the milk and add salt and pepper to taste. Transfer the mashed potatoes to the baking dish.

DRAIN the scorzonera and allow them to drain well. Place the scorzonera, asparagus, or endive on the mashed potatoes and top with the crème fraiche mixture.

BAKE the casserole in the preheated oven for about 20 minutes until golden brown.

Preparation time: 30 minutes
Baking time: 20 minutes

INDEX

A

Apple
Sauerkraut casserole with red wine, apple, brie and thyme **88**
Apple syrup
Onion stew with abbey beer, apple syrup, and fennel seeds **237**
Aromatic couscous with eggplant, chickpeas, and tomato 20
Arroz meloso with dry-cured olives and green asparagus 219
Artichoke
Crunchy artichokes with olive mayonnaise **210**
Arugula
Beet and potato mash with arugula and crispy goat cheese **48**
Butternut squash Wellington with barrel-aged feta **201**
Gratin dauphinois with sweet potato and arugulaginger salsa **206**
Rotolo with roasted green asparagus **224**
Slow-cooked pumpkin confit with creamy cheese and crisp basil **202**
Asparagus
Arroz meloso with dry-cured olives and green asparagus **219**
Capunsei with baby asparagus and lemon gremolata **218**
Roasted white asparagus with poached egg and parsley butter **226**
Rotolo with roasted green asparagus **224**
Avocado
Sushi balls with marinated avocado **103**
Sushi roll with edamame and green chili-lime mayonnaise **115**

B

Baked eggplant with whipped goat cheese and poppy seeds 10
Baked endive with walnuts and rosemary crumble 179
Barbecued Romano peppers with marinated feta 198
Basil
Eggs in tomato-ginger sauce **166**
Chickpea balls in tomato sauce **93**
Hearty herb and lemon balls with Parmesan **106**
Lemon-ricotta balls with saffron cream **108**
Lentil ragu with red wine and basil **144**
Olive ragu with cherry tomatoes, polenta, and crispy basil **184**
Pesto **143**
Ravioli with tomato-mascarpone sauce and basil **187**
Risotto with honey-drizzled tomatoes and buffalo ricotta **197**
Seared zucchini with Parmesan-basil hollandaise **38**
Slow-cooked pumpkin confit with creamy cheese and crisp basil **202**
Spaghetti with purple-podded peas and cream, Parmesan, and lemon **136**
Stuffed beefsteak tomatoes with lime ricotta and herb pesto **196**
Stuffed zucchini with herbed ricotta in puff pastry **41**
Basil, red
Thai yellow curry with roasted vegetables **30**
Beans
Cajun rice with bell pepper and tomato **188**
Cannellini bean purée with crème fraiche **148**
Giant leek lumpia with bean sprouts, omelet, and edamame **233**
Giant white beans in tomato sauce with red wine, coriander seeds, and rosemary **147**
Lentil and bean tagine with cherry tomatoes and lime-infused yogurt **141**
Pearl couscous with fava beans and cilantro salsa verde, orange, and smoked almonds **116**
Tagliatelle with spinach, cannellini beans, and pesto **145**
Bean sprout omelet with sweet-and-sour ginger sauce and shiitake mushrooms 122
Bean sprouts
Bean sprout omelet with sweet-and-sour ginger sauce and shiitake mushrooms **122**
Giant leek lumpia with bean sprouts, omelet, and edamame **233**
Béchamel
Mini-cannelloni with roasted sweet potatoes and buffalo mozzarella **213**
Mushroom lasagna with Parmesan béchamel sauce **126**
Beer
Belgian endive with beer, honey, and thyme **176**
Onion stew with abbey beer, apple syrup, and fennel seeds **237**
Beet and potato mash with arugula and crispy goat cheese 48
Beet and quinoa burger with truffle sauce 63
Beet dumplings with green onions 58
Beet gnocchi with whipped ricotta and crispy sage 62
Beets
Beet and quinoa burger with truffle sauce **63**
Beet and potato mash with arugula and crispy goat cheese **48**

Beet dumplings with green onions **58**
Beet gnocchi with whipped ricotta and crispy sage **62**
Beet tartare with soy sauce and sriracha **52**
Fresh beet noodles with shiitake and sesame **45**
Hasselback beets with thyme and feta **55**
Marinated beets with lime, coriander and yogurt **59**
Sweet-and-sour beets with rice vinegar and ginger **44**
Tian of beet with red sage and smoked sea salt **53**
Beet tartare with soy sauce and sriracha 52
Belgian endive with beer, honey, and thyme 176
Black garlic
Kale risotto with black garlic and crispy kale **84**
Brie
Sauerkraut casserole with red wine, apple, Brie, and thyme **88**
Broccoli
Tray bake with broccoli, baby potatoes, and Vacherin Mont d'Or **74**
Brussels sprouts
Charred Brussels sprouts with crème fraiche and pickled chili pepper **82**
Hash browns with Brussels sprouts and mushrooms **83**
Burrata
Truffle risotto with mushrooms and mini burrata **123**
Butternut squash
Butternut squash Wellington with barrel-aged feta **201**
Hasselback butternut squash with beurre noisette mayonnaise **205**
Butternut squash Wellington with barrel-aged feta 201

C

Cabbage, green
Roasted vegetable pithiviers and Parmesan sauce **192**
Cabbage, pointed
Fried rice with pointed cabbage and red-skinned peanuts **87**
Pointed cabbage curry with sesame **78**
Cabbage, red
Red cabbage teriyaki with star anise and sesame seeds **71**
Cajun rice with bell pepper and tomato 188
Camembert
Warm camembert with lemon and thyme **220**
Cannellini bean purée with crème fraiche 148
Cannelloni
Mini-cannelloni with roasted sweet potatoes and buffalo mozzarella **213**
Capers
Haricots verts (thin green beans) with chili and caper salsa **112**
Pearl couscous with fava beans and cilantro salsa verde, orange, and smoked almonds **116**
Capunsei with baby asparagus and lemon gremolata 218
Cauliflower
Cauliflower quiche with cheese and tarragon **68**
Cauliflower tempura with spicy mango sauce **67**
Roasted cauliflower curry with cilantro **66**
Cauliflower quiche with cheese and tarragon 68
Cauliflower tempura with spicy mango sauce 67
Celery root
Pan-fried celery root with creamy pepper sauce **245**
Vegetarian split pea soup with dried mushrooms **158**
Celery stalk
Cajun rice with bell pepper and tomato **188**
Lentil ragu with red wine and basil **144**
Olive ragu with cherry tomatoes, polenta, and crispy basil **184**
Polenta and spinach gratin with Gorgonzola and pine nuts **170**
Charred Brussels sprouts with crème fraiche and pickled chili pepper 82
Chickpea and tomato balls 90
Chickpea balls in tomato sauce 93
Chickpeas
Aromatic couscous with eggplant, chickpeas, and tomato **20**
Chickpea and tomato balls **90**
Chickpea balls in tomato sauce **93**
Chickpea stew with Romano peppers and dates **150**
Chickpeas with spinach in vadouvan sauce **157**
Thai red curry with chickpeas, ginger, and cilantro **153**
Chickpea stew with Romano peppers and dates 150
Chickpeas with spinach in vadouvan sauce 157
Chili flakes

Butternut squash Wellington with barrel-aged feta **201**
Chili oil with garlic **230**
Gnocchi with cavolo nero, fennel seeds, and pecorino **75**
Hearty herb and lemon balls with Parmesan **106**
Marinated tofu **95**
Whole-wheat lasagna with lentils and mozzarella crème **156**

Chili oil
Chili oil with garlic **230**
Ravioli with tomato-mascarpone sauce and basil **187**

Chili sauce, sweet
Eggs in chili-peanut sauce **165**
Fresh beet noodles with shiitake and sesame **45**
Giant leek lumpia with bean sprouts, omelet, and edamame **233**
Roasted zucchini with chili soy sauce and sesame **37**
Sushi roll with edamame and green chili-lime mayonnaise **115**

Chives
Hearty herb and lemon balls with Parmesan **106**
Stuffed zucchini with herbed ricotta in puff pastry **41**

Cilantro
Flatbread with lime, cilantro, and garlic **28**
Pearl couscous with fava beans and cilantro salsa verde, orange, and smoked almonds **116**
Pointed cabbage curry with sesame **78**
Roasted cauliflower curry with cilantro **66**
Thai red curry with chickpeas, ginger, and cilantro **153**

Coconut milk
Eggs in chili-peanut sauce **165**
Eggs in green curry sauce **163**
Green curry with sugar snap peas, tofu, and sticky peanuts **111**
Pointed cabbage curry with sesame **78**
Roasted cauliflower curry with cilantro **66**
Thai red curry with chickpeas, ginger, and cilantro **153**
Thai yellow curry with roasted vegetables **30**

Comté
Creamy leeks with mustard and Comté **234**

Corn
Roasted sweet corn with garlicky yogurt and olive herb **209**

Cornstarch
Cauliflower tempura with spicy mango sauce **67**

Couscous
Aromatic couscous with eggplant, chickpeas, and tomato **20**
Harissa couscous with roasted vegetables **31**
Pearl couscous with fava beans and cilantro salsa verde, orange, and smoked almonds **116**

Creamy leeks with mustard and Comté 234
Creamy mushroom pot pie with Riesling 129
Creamy parsnip gratin with oregano 244
Crème fraiche
Cannellini bean purée with crème fraiche **148**
Creamy leeks with mustard and Comté **234**
Creamy parsnip gratin with oregano **244**
Sauerkraut casserole with red wine, apple, Brie, and thyme **88**
Scorzonera casserole with mashed potatoes and herbed crème fraiche **248**

Curry paste
Eggs in green curry sauce **163**
Green curry with sugar snap peas, tofu, and sticky peanuts **111**
Pointed cabbage curry with sesame **78**
Roasted cauliflower curry with cilantro **66**
Thai eggplant-rice croquettes with lime and cilantro **14**
Thai red curry with chickpeas, ginger, and cilantro **153**
Thai yellow curry paste **25**
Thai yellow curry with roasted vegetables **30**

Crispy baby potatoes with lemon and rosemary 96
Crispy lentil-truffle balls with truffle-Parmesan mayonnaise 107
Crunchy artichokes with olive mayonnaise 210
Crunchy baked spinach with cream, Emmentaler, and lemon 169
Crunchy eggplant with harissa oil and thyme 34

D
Dates
Chickpea stew with Romano peppers and dates **150**
Dill
Flatbread with yogurt and dill **28**
Goat labneh with muhammara and dill **33**

Stuffed beefsteak tomatoes with lime ricotta and herb pesto **196**
Dutch blue cheese
Swiss chard and potato mash with mushrooms **175**

E
Edamame
Giant leek lumpia with bean sprouts, omelet and edamame **233**
Sushi roll with edamame and green chili-lime mayonnaise **115**

Eggplant
Aromatic couscous with eggplant, chickpeas, and tomato **20**
Baked eggplant with whipped goat cheese and poppy seeds **10**
Crunchy eggplant with harissa oil and thyme **34**
Eggplant balls in hoisin-ginger sauce **99**
Eggplant satay with ginger and peanut sauce **18**
Indonesian-inspired eggplant with tomato and sweet soy sauce **13**
Stifatho with eggplant and Kalamata olives **23**
Thai eggplant-rice croquettes with lime and cilantro **14**
Thai yellow curry with roasted vegetables **30**

Eggplant balls in hoisin-ginger sauce 99
Eggplant satay with ginger and peanut sauce 18
Egg roll
Giant leek lumpia with bean sprouts, omelet, and edamame **233**

Eggs
Bean sprouts omelet with sweet-and-sour ginger sauce and shiitake mushrooms **122**
Beet and potato mash with arugula and crispy goat cheese **48**
Cauliflower quiche with cheese and tarragon **68**
Eggs in chili-peanut sauce **165**
Eggs in green curry sauce **163**
Eggs in red wine sauce **164**
Eggs in soy sauce **162**
Eggs in stroganoff sauce **167**
Eggs in tomato-ginger sauce **166**
Roasted white asparagus with poached egg and parsley butter **226**
Skillet quiche with leafy green vegetables, ricotta, and Parmesan **174**

Eggs in chili-peanut sauce 165
Eggs in green curry sauce 163
Eggs in red wine sauce 164
Eggs in soy sauce 162
Eggs in stroganoff sauce 167
Eggs in tomato-ginger sauce 166
Emmentaler
Creamy parsnip gratin with oregano **244**
Crunchy baked spinach with cream, Swiss cheese and lemon **169**
Endive
Baked endive with walnuts and rosemary crumble **179**
Belgian endive with beer, honey, and thyme **176**
Scorzonera casserole with mashed potatoes and herbed crème fraiche **248**

F
Fennel
Pasta al cartoccio with braised fennel and Stilton **229**
Fennel seeds
Beet gnocchi with whipped ricotta and crispy sage **62**
Gnocchi with cavolo nero, fennel seeds, and pecorino **75**
Olive ragu with cherry tomatoes, polenta, and crispy basil **184**
Onion stew with abbey beer, apple syrup, and fennel seeds **237**
Feta
Barbecued Romano peppers with marinated feta **198**
Butternut squash Wellington with barrel-aged feta **201**
Hasselback beets with thyme and feta **55**
Roasted feta with olives, lemon honey, and thyme **125**

Flatbread 27
Flatbread with beet and cumin 28
Flatbread with lime, cilantro, and garlic 28
Flatbread with tomato 28
Flatbread with yogurt and dill 28
Fresh beet noodles with shiitake and sesame 45
Fresh plain noodles 47
Fresh toasted, spiced coconut 18
Fried rice with pointed cabbage and red-skinned peanuts 87
Fried tofu crumbles 95

G
Giant leek lumpia with bean sprouts, omelet, and edamame 233
Giant white beans in tomato sauce with red wine, coriander seeds,

and rosemary 147
Ginger
  Bean sprout omelet with sweet-and-sour ginger sauce
  and shiitake mushrooms 122
  Eggplant balls in hoisin-ginger sauce 99
  Eggplant satay with ginger and peanut sauce 18
  Eggs in tomato-ginger sauce 166
  Gratin dauphinois with sweet potato and arugula-ginger salsa 206
  Shiitake mushrooms with ginger, sriracha, and green onion 133
  Sweet-and-sour beets with rice vinegar and ginger 44
  Sushi balls with marinated avocado 103
  Sushi roll with edamame and green chili-lime mayonnaise 115
  Thai red curry with chickpeas, ginger, and cilantro 153
  Thai yellow curry paste 25
Ginger syrup
  Bean sprouts omelet with sweet-and-sour ginger sauce and shiitake
  mushrooms 122
  Gratin dauphinois with sweet potato and arugula-ginger salsa 206
  Green curry with sugar snap peas, tofu, and sticky peanuts 111
  Shiitake mushrooms with ginger, sriracha, and green onion 133
Gnocchi
  Beet gnocchi with whipped ricotta and crispy sage 62
  Capunsei with baby asparagus and lemon gremolata 218
  Gnocchi with cavolo nero, fennel seeds, and pecorino 75
Gnocchi with cavolo nero, fennel seeds, and pecorino 75
Goat cheese
  Baked eggplant with whipped goat cheese and poppy seeds 10
  Beet and potato mash with arugula and crispy goat cheese 48
  Portobello mushrooms with spinach, goat cheese, and easy onion jam 130
  Roasted sweet corn with garlicky yogurt and olive herb 209
  Slow-cooked pumpkin confit with creamy cheese and crisp basil 202
Goat labneh with muhammara and dill 33
Gorgonzola
  Kale risotto with black garlic and crispy kale 84
  Polenta and spinach gratin with Gorgonzola and pine nuts 170
Gouda
  Baked endive with walnuts and rosemary crumble 179
  Cauliflower quiche with cheese and tarragon 68
  Scorzonera casserole with mashed potatoes and herbed crème fraiche 248
Gratin dauphinois with sweet potato and arugula-ginger salsa 206
Green beans
  Haricots verts (thin green beans) with chili and caper salsa 112
  Thai yellow curry with roasted vegetables 30
Green curry with sugar snap peas, tofu, and sticky peanuts 111
Green onion
  Bean sprout omelet with sweet-and-sour ginger sauce and shiitake
  mushrooms 122
  Beet dumplings with green onions 58
  Cajun rice with bell pepper and tomato 188
  Eggplant balls in hoisin-ginger sauce 99
  Green curry with sugar snap peas, tofu, and sticky peanuts 111
  Hash browns with Brussels sprouts and mushrooms 83
  Shiitake mushrooms with ginger, sriracha, and green onion 133
Ground meat (vegetarian)
  Beet dumplings with green onions 58
  Hearty herb and lemon balls with Parmesan 106
Gruyère
  Gratin dauphinois with sweet potato and arugula-ginger salsa 206

H
Haricots verts (thin green beans) with chili and caper salsa 112
Harissa
  Crunchy eggplant with harissa oil and thyme 34
  Harissa couscous with roasted vegetables 31
Harissa couscous with roasted vegetables 31
Hash browns with Brussels sprouts and mushrooms 83
Hasselback beets with thyme and feta 55
Hasselback butternut squash with beurre noisette mayonnaise 205
Hearty herb and lemon balls with Parmesan 106
Hoisin
  Eggplant balls in hoisin-ginger sauce 99
Honey
  Belgian endive with beer, honey, and thyme 176
  Risotto with honey-drizzled tomatoes and buffalo ricotta 197

  Roasted feta with olives, lemon honey, and thyme 125
  Marinated tofu 95
I
Indonesian-inspired eggplant with tomato and sweet soy sauce 13
J
Jerusalem artichoke gratin with magor and Parmesan 247
K
Kale
  Gnocchi with cavolo nero, fennel seeds, and pecorino 75
  Kale risotto with black garlic and crispy kale 84
L
Lasagna sheets
  Mini-cannelloni with roasted sweet potatoes and buffalo mozzarella 213
  Mushroom lasagna with Parmesan béchamel sauce 126
  Whole-wheat lasagna with lentils and mozzarella crème 156
Leek
  Creamy leeks with mustard and Comté 234
  Giant leek lumpia with bean sprouts, omelet, and edamame 233
Lemon
  Arroz meloso with dry-cured olives and green asparagus 219
  Barbecued Romano peppers with marinated feta 198
  Capunsei with baby asparagus and lemon gremolata 218
  Crispy baby potatoes with lemon and rosemary 96
  Crunchy artichokes with olive mayonnaise 210
  Crunchy baked spinach with cream, Emmentaler, and lemon 169
  Hearty herb and lemon balls with Parmesan 106
  Lemon-ricotta balls with saffron cream 108
  Pearl couscous with fava beans and cilantro salsa verde, orange, and
  smoked almonds 116
  Roasted feta with olives, lemon honey, and thyme 125
  Rotolo with roasted green asparagus 224
  Seared zucchini with Parmesan-basil hollandaise 38
  Spaghetti with purple-podded peas and cream, Parmesan, and lemon 136
  Stuffed zucchini with herbed ricotta in puff pastry 41
  Tomato and bell pepper paella with purple-podded peas 185
  Warm camembert with lemon and thyme 220
Lemon-ricotta balls with saffron cream 108
Lentil and bean tagine with cherry tomatoes and lime-infused yogurt 141
Lentil ragu with red wine and basil 144
Lentils
  Crispy lentil-truffle balls with truffle-Parmesan mayonnaise 107
  Lentil and bean tagine with cherry tomatoes and lime-infused yogurt 141
  Lentil ragu with red wine and basil 144
  Whole-wheat lasagna with lentils and mozzarella crème 156
M
Magor
  Jerusalem artichoke gratin with magor and Parmesan 247
Mango
  Cauliflower tempura with spicy mango sauce 67
Marinated beets with lime, coriander seeds, and yogurt 59
Marinated tofu 95
Mascarpone
  Ravioli with tomato-mascarpone sauce and basil 187
Mayonnaise
  Beet and quinoa burger with truffle sauce 63
  Crispy lentil-truffle balls with truffle-Parmesan mayonnaise 107
  Crunchy artichokes with olive mayonnaise 210
  Hasselback butternut squash with beurre noisette mayonnaise 205
  Sushi balls with marinated avocado 103
  Sushi roll with edamame and green chili-lime mayonnaise 115
Mini-cannelloni with roasted sweet potatoes and buffalo mozzarella 213
Mozzarella
  Mini-cannelloni with roasted sweet potatoes and buffalo mozzarella 213
  Mushroom lasagna with Parmesan béchamel sauce 126
  Rotolo with roasted green asparagus 224
  Smoked buffalo mozzarella 138
  Whole-wheat lasagna with lentils and mozzarella crème 156
Mushroom, assorted
  Creamy mushroom pot pie with Riesling 129
  Eggs in stroganoff sauce 167
  Swiss chard and potato mash with mushrooms 175
  Truffle risotto with mushrooms and mini burrata 123

Mushroom, button
Giant white beans in tomato sauce with red wine, coriander seeds, and rosemary **147**

Mushroom, cremini
Crispy lentil-truffle balls with truffle-Parmesan mayonnaise **107**
Eggs in stroganoff sauce **167**
Hash browns with Brussels sprouts and mushrooms **83**
Mushroom lasagna with Parmesan béchamel sauce **126**

Mushroom, dried
Mushroom lasagna with Parmesan béchamel sauce **126**
Vegetarian split pea soup with dried mushrooms **158**

Mushroom lasagna with Parmesan béchamel sauce 126

Mushroom, portobello
Portobello mushrooms with spinach, goat cheese, and easy onion jam **130**

Mushroom, shiitake
Bean sprout omelet with sweet-and-sour ginger sauce and shiitake mushrooms **122**
Fresh beet noodles with shiitake and sesame **45**
Mushroom lasagna with Parmesan béchamel sauce **126**
Shiitake mushrooms with ginger, sriracha, and green onion **133**

Mustard
Beet tartare with soy sauce and sriracha **52**
Creamy leeks with mustard and Comté **234**
Creamy parsnip gratin with oregano **244**
Hasselback butternut squash with beurre noisette mayonnaise **205**
Sushi roll with edamame and green chili-lime mayonnaise **115**

N

Noodles
Fresh beet noodles with shiitake and sesame **45**
Fresh plain noodles **47**
Thai red curry with chickpeas, ginger, and cilantro **153**

O

Olive ragu with cherry tomatoes, polenta, and crispy basil 184

Olives
Arroz meloso with dry-cured olives and green asparagus **219**
Crunchy artichokes with olive mayonnaise **210**
Lentil and bean tagine with cherry tomatoes and lime-infused yogurt **141**
Olive ragu with cherry tomatoes, polenta, and crispy basil **184**
Roasted feta with olives, lemon honey, and thyme **125**
Stifatho with eggplant and Kalamata olives **23**

Onion
Harissa couscous with roasted vegetables **31**
Onion stew with abbey beer, apple syrup, and fennel seeds **237**
Portobello mushrooms with spinach, goat cheese, and easy onion jam **130**
Stewed onions shepherd's pie with rosemary **238**
Tray bake with broccoli, baby potatoes, and Vacherin Mont d'Or **74**

Onion, red
Harissa couscous with roasted vegetables **31**
Roasted vegetable pithiviers and Parmesan sauce **192**
Tray bake with broccoli, baby potatoes, and Vacherin Mont d'Or **74**

Onion stew with abbey beer, apple syrup, and fennel seeds 237

Orange
Pearl couscous with fava beans and cilantro salsa verde, orange, and smoked almonds **116**
Slow-cooked pumpkin confit with creamy cheese and crisp basil **202**

Oregano
Creamy parsnip gratin with oregano **244**
Roasted feta with olives, lemon honey, and thyme **125**
Roasted vegetable pithiviers and Parmesan sauce **192**
Whole-wheat lasagna with lentils and mozzarella crème **156**

P

Paella
Tomato and bell pepper paella with purple-podded peas **185**

Pan-fried celery root with creamy pepper sauce 245

Parmesan
Capunsei with baby asparagus and lemon gremolata **218**
Crispy lentil-truffle balls with truffle-Parmesan mayonnaise **107**
Hearty herb and lemon balls with Parmesan **106**
Jerusalem artichoke gratin with magor and Parmesan **247**
Lemon-ricotta balls with saffron cream **108**
Lentil ragu with red wine and basil **144**
Mini-cannelloni with roasted sweet potatoes and buffalo mozzarella **213**
Mushroom lasagna with Parmesan béchamel sauce **126**
Olive ragu with cherry tomatoes, polenta, and crispy basil **184**

Polenta balls with wild garlic in smoky tomato sauce **100**
Roasted vegetable pithiviers and Parmesan sauce **192**
Seared zucchini with Parmesan-basil hollandaise **38**
Skillet quiche with leafy green vegetables, ricotta, and Parmesan **174**
Spaghetti with purple-podded peas and cream, Parmesan, and lemon **136**
Stuffed beefsteak tomatoes with lime ricotta and herb pesto **196**
Stuffed zucchini with herbed ricotta in puff pastry **41**
Tagliatelle with spinach, cannellini beans, and pesto **145**
Whole-wheat lasagna with lentils and mozzarella crème **156**

Parsley
Arroz meloso with dry-cured olives and green asparagus **219**
Cajun rice with bell pepper and tomato **188**
Capunsei with baby asparagus and lemon gremolata **218**
Cauliflower tempura with spicy mango sauce **67**
Creamy leeks with mustard and Comté **234**
Creamy mushroom pot pie with Riesling **129**
Crunchy artichokes with olive mayonnaise **210**
Eggs in stroganoff sauce **167**
Harissa couscous with roasted vegetables **31**
Hearty herb and lemon balls with Parmesan **106**
Lentil and bean tagine with cherry tomatoes and lime-infused yogurt **141**
Pan-fried celery root with creamy pepper sauce **245**
Red cabbage teriyaki with star anise and sesame seeds **71**
Roasted white asparagus with poached egg and parsley butter **226**
Stuffed beefsteak tomatoes with lime ricotta and herb pesto **196**
Tomato and bell pepper paella with purple-podded peas **185**

Parsnip
Creamy parsnip gratin with oregano **244**
Stewed onions shepherd's pie with rosemary **238**

Pasta
Lentil ragu with red wine and basil **144**
Mini-cannelloni with roasted sweet potatoes and buffalo mozzarella **213**
Mushroom lasagna with Parmesan béchamel sauce **126**
Pasta al cartoccio with braised fennel and Stilton **229**
Ravioli with tomato-mascarpone sauce and basil **187**
Rotolo with roasted green asparagus **224**
Spaghetti with purple-podded peas and cream, Parmesan, and lemon **136**
Tagliatelle with spinach, cannellini beans, and pesto **145**
Whole-wheat lasagna with lentils and mozzarella crème **156**

Pasta al cartoccio with braised fennel and Stilton 229

Peanut butter with sea salt 19

Peanuts
Eggplant satay with ginger and peanut sauce **18**
Eggs in chili-peanut sauce **165**
Fresh toasted, spiced coconut **18**
Fried rice with pointed cabbage and red-skinned peanuts **87**
Green curry with sugar snap peas, tofu, and sticky peanuts **111**
Peanut butter with sea salt **19**

Pearl couscous with fava beans and cilantro salsa verde, orange, and smoked almonds 116

Peas
Green curry with sugar snap peas, tofu, and sticky peanuts **111**
Spaghetti with purple-podded peas and cream, Parmesan, and lemon **136**
Tomato and bell pepper paella with purple-podded peas **185**
Vegetarian split pea soup with dried mushrooms **158**

Pecorino
Gnocchi with cavolo nero, fennel seeds, and pecorino **75**

Pepper, bell
Bean sprout omelet with sweet-and-sour ginger sauce and shiitake mushrooms **122**
Cajun rice with bell pepper and tomato **188**
Eggs in stroganoff sauce **167**
Green curry with sugar snap peas, tofu, and sticky peanuts **111**
Harissa couscous with roasted vegetables **31**
Roasted vegetable pithiviers and Parmesan sauce **192**
Thai yellow curry with roasted vegetables **30**
Tomato and bell pepper paella with purple-podded peas **185**

Peppercorn
Beet tartare with soy sauce and sriracha **52**
Pan-fried celery root with creamy pepper sauce **245**

Pepper, red chili
Charred Brussels sprouts with crème fraiche and pickled chili pepper **82**
Haricots verts (thin green beans) with chili and caper salsa **112**
Roasted zucchini with chili soy sauce and sesame **37**
Thai yellow curry paste **25**

Pepper, Romano
Barbecued Romano peppers with marinated feta **198**
Chickpea stew with Romano peppers and dates **150**
Roasted cauliflower curry with cilantro **66**
Sauerkraut casserole with red wine, apple, Brie, and thyme **88**
Thai red curry with chickpeas, ginger, and cilantro **153**
Pesto 143
Tagliatelle with spinach, cannellini beans, and pesto **145**
Pointed cabbage curry with sesame 78
Polenta
Olive ragu with cherry tomatoes, polenta, and crispy basil **184**
Polenta and spinach gratin with Gorgonzola and pine nuts **170**
Polenta balls with wild garlic in smoky tomato sauce **100**
Polenta and spinach gratin with Gorgonzola and pine nuts 170
Polenta balls with wild garlic in smoky tomato sauce 100
Portobello mushrooms with spinach, goat cheese, and easy onion jam 130
Potatoes
Beet and potato mash with arugula and crispy goat cheese **48**
Beet gnocchi with whipped ricotta and crispy sage **62**
Crispy baby potatoes with lemon and rosemary **96**
Gratin dauphinois with sweet potato and arugula-ginger salsa **206**
Hash browns with Brussels sprouts and mushrooms **83**
Sauerkraut casserole with red wine, apple, Brie, and thyme **88**
Scorzonera casserole with mashed potatoes and herbed crème fraiche **248**
Stewed onions shepherd's pie with rosemary **238**
Swiss chard and potato mash with mushrooms **175**
Tray bake with broccoli, baby potatoes, and Vacherin Mont d'Or **74**
Vegetarian split pea soup with dried mushrooms **158**
Puff pastry
Butternut squash Wellington with barrel-aged feta **201**
Cauliflower quiche with cheese and tarragon **68**
Creamy mushroom pot pie with Riesling **129**
Roasted vegetable pithiviers and Parmesan sauce **192**
Skillet quiche with leafy green vegetables, ricotta, and Parmesan **174**
Stuffed zucchini with herbed ricotta in puff pastry **41**
Pumpkin
Roasted vegetable pithiviers and Parmesan sauce **192**
Slow-cooked pumpkin confit with creamy cheese and crisp basil **202**

Q
Quiche
Cauliflower quiche with cheese and tarragon **68**
Skillet quiche with leafy vegetables, ricotta, and Parmesan cheese **174**
Quinoa
Beet and quinoa burger with truffle sauce **63**

R
Ragu
Lentil ragu with red wine and basil **144**
Olive ragu with cherry tomatoes, polenta, and crispy basil **184**
Ravioli with tomato-mascarpone sauce and basil 187
Red cabbage teriyaki with star anise and sesame seeds 71
Rice
Arroz meloso with dry-cured olives and green asparagus **219**
Cajun rice with bell pepper and tomato **188**
Fried rice with pointed cabbage and red-skinned peanuts **87**
Green curry with sugar snap peas, tofu, and sticky peanuts **111**
Indonesian-inspired eggplant with tomato and sweet soy sauce **13**
Roasted cauliflower curry with cilantro **66**
Shiitake mushrooms with ginger, sriracha, and green onion **133**
Sushi balls with marinated avocado **103**
Sushi roll with edamame and green chili-lime mayonnaise **115**
Thai eggplant-rice croquettes with lime and cilantro **14**
Thai yellow curry with roasted vegetables **30**
Tomato and bell pepper paella with purple-podded peas **185**
Ricotta
Beet gnocchi with whipped ricotta and crispy sage **62**
Lemon-ricotta balls with saffron cream **108**
Mini-cannelloni with roasted sweet potatoes and buffalo mozzarella **213**
Risotto with honey-drizzled tomatoes and buffalo ricotta **197**
Rotolo with roasted green asparagus **224**
Skillet quiche with leafy green vegetables, ricotta, and Parmesan **174**
Stuffed beefsteak tomatoes with lime ricotta and herb pesto **196**
Stuffed zucchini with herbed ricotta in puff pastry **41**

Riesling
Creamy mushroom pot pie with Riesling **129**
Risotto
Kale risotto with black garlic and crispy kale **84**
Risotto with honey-drizzled tomatoes and buffalo ricotta **197**
Truffle risotto with mushrooms and mini burrata **123**
Risotto with honey-drizzled tomatoes and buffalo ricotta 197
Roasted cauliflower curry with cilantro 66
Roasted feta with olives, lemon honey, and thyme 125
Roasted sweet corn with garlicky yogurt and olive herb 209
Roasted vegetable pithiviers and Parmesan sauce 192
Roasted white asparagus with poached egg and parsley butter 226
Roasted zucchini with chili soy sauce and sesame 37
Rotolo with roasted green asparagus 224

S
Saffron
Lemon-ricotta balls with saffron cream **108**
Tomato and bell pepper paella with purple-podded peas **185**
Sambal
Eggplant satay with ginger and peanut sauce **18**
Fried rice with pointed cabbage and red-skinned peanuts **87**
Indonesian-inspired eggplant with tomato and sweet soy sauce **13**
Sauerkraut casserole with red wine, apple, Brie, and thyme 88
Scorzonera casserole with mashed potatoes and herbed crème fraiche 248
Seared zucchini with Parmesan-basil hollandaise 38
Shiitake mushrooms with ginger, sriracha, and green onion 133
Skillet quiche with leafy green vegetables, ricotta, and Parmesan 174
Slow-cooked pumpkin confit with creamy cheese and crisp basil 202
Smoked buffalo mozzarella 138
Soy sauce
Beet tartare with soy sauce and sriracha **52**
Eggplant balls in hoisin-ginger sauce **99**
Marinated tofu **95**
Roasted zucchini with chili soy sauce and sesame **37**
Shiitake mushrooms with ginger, sriracha, and green onion **133**
Sushi balls with marinated avocado **103**
Sushi roll with edamame and green chili-lime mayonnaise **115**
Teriyaki sauce **71**
Soy sauce, sweet
Eggplant satay with ginger and peanut sauce **18**
Eggs in chili-peanut sauce **165**
Eggs in soy sauce **162**
Fried rice with pointed cabbage and red-skinned peanuts **87**
Indonesian-inspired eggplant with tomato and sweet soy sauce **13**
Spaghetti
Lentil ragu with red wine and basil **144**
Spaghetti with purple-podded peas and cream, Parmesan, and lemon **136**
Spaghetti with purple-podded peas and cream, Parmesan, and lemon 136
Spinach
Chickpeas with spinach in vadouvan sauce **157**
Crunchy baked spinach with cream, Emmentaler, and lemon **169**
Jerusalem artichoke gratin with magor and Parmesan **247**
Polenta and spinach gratin with Gorgonzola and pine nuts **170**
Portobello mushrooms with spinach, goat cheese, and easy onion jam **130**
Skillet quiche with leafy green vegetables, ricotta, and Parmesan **174**
Tagliatelle with spinach, cannellini beans, and pesto **145**
Split peas
Vegetarian split pea soup with dried mushrooms **158**
Sriracha
Beet tartare with soy sauce and sriracha **52**
Cauliflower tempura with spicy mango sauce **67**
Shiitake mushrooms with ginger, sriracha, and green onion **133**
Stewed onions shepherd's pie with rosemary 238
Stifatho with eggplant and Kalamata olives 23
Stilton
Pasta al cartoccio with braised fennel and Stilton **229**
Stuffed beefsteak tomatoes with lime ricotta and herb pesto 196
Stuffed zucchini with herbed ricotta in puff pastry 41
Sugar snap peas
Green curry with sugar snap peas, tofu, and sticky peanuts **111**
Sushi balls with marinated avocado 103
Sushi roll with edamame and green chili-lime mayonnaise 115
Sweet-and-sour beets with rice vinegar and ginger 44

Sweet potatoes
  Gratin dauphinois with sweet potato and arugula-ginger salsa **206**
  Mini-cannelloni with roasted sweet potatoes and buffalo mozzarella **213**
  Thai yellow curry with roasted vegetables **30**
Swiss chard
  Skillet quiche with leafy green vegetables, ricotta, and Parmesan **174**
  Swiss chard and potato mash with mushrooms **175**
Swiss chard and potato mash with mushrooms 175

T
Tagliatelle
  Pasta al cartoccio with braised fennel and Stilton **229**
  Tagliatelle with spinach, cannellini beans, and pesto **145**
Tagliatelle with spinach, cannellini beans, and pesto 145
Teriyaki sauce 71
  Red cabbage teriyaki with star anise and sesame seeds **71**
Thai eggplant-rice croquettes with lime and cilantro 14
Thai red curry with chickpeas, ginger, and cilantro 153
Thai yellow curry paste 25
Thai yellow curry with roasted vegetables 30
Thyme
  Baked eggplant with whipped goat cheese and poppy seeds **10**
  Barbecued Romano peppers with marinated feta **198**
  Belgian endive with beer, honey, and thyme **176**
  Cannellini bean purée with crème fraiche **148**
  Crunchy eggplant with harissa oil and thyme **34**
  Eggs in red wine sauce **164**
  Hasselback beets with thyme and feta **55**
  Hasselback butternut squash with beurre noisette mayonnaise **205**
  Mini-cannelloni with roasted sweet potatoes and buffalo mozzarella **213**
  Mushroom lasagna with Parmesan béchamel sauce **126**
  Roasted feta with olives, lemon honey, and thyme **125**
  Roasted sweet corn with garlicky yogurt and olive herb **209**
  Roasted vegetable pithiviers and Parmesan sauce **192**
  Sauerkraut casserole with red wine, apple, Brie, and thyme **88**
  Skillet quiche with leafy green vegetables, ricotta, and Parmesan **174**
  Vegetarian split pea soup with dried mushrooms **158**
  Warm camembert with lemon and thyme **220**
Tian of beet with red sage and smoked sea salt 53
Tofu
  Fried tofu crumbles **95**
  Green curry with sugar snap peas, tofu, and sticky peanuts **111**
  Marinated tofu **95**
Tomato and bell pepper paella with purple-podded peas 185
Tomatoes
  Aromatic couscous with eggplant, chickpeas, and tomato **20**
  Chickpea balls in tomato sauce **93**
  Chickpea stew with Romano peppers and dates **150**
  Crunchy eggplant with harissa oil and thyme **34**
  Eggs in tomato-ginger sauce **166**
  Giant white beans in tomato sauce with red wine, coriander seeds, and rosemary **147**
  Indonesian-inspired eggplant with tomato and sweet soy sauce **13**
  Lentil ragu with red wine and basil **144**
  Mushroom lasagna with Parmesan béchamel sauce **126**
  Polenta balls with wild garlic in smoky tomato sauce **100**
  Ravioli with tomato-mascarpone sauce and basil **187**
  Rotolo with roasted green asparagus **224**
  Stifatho with eggplant and Kalamata olives **23**
  Stuffed beefsteak tomatoes with lime ricotta and herb pesto **196**
  Tomato and bell pepper paella with purple-podded peas **185**
  Whole-wheat lasagna with lentils and mozzarella crème **156**
Tomatoes, cherry
  Cajun rice with bell pepper and tomato **188**
  Lentil and bean tagine with cherry tomatoes and lime-infused yogurt **141**
  Mini-cannelloni with roasted sweet potatoes and buffalo mozzarella **213**
  Mushroom lasagna with Parmesan béchamel sauce **126**
  Olive ragu with cherry tomatoes, polenta, and crispy basil **184**
  Risotto with honey-drizzled tomatoes and buffalo ricotta **197**
Tomatoes, semi-dried
  Chickpea and tomato balls **90**
  Pasta al cartoccio with braised fennel and Stilton **229**
  Portobello mushrooms with spinach, goat cheese, and easy onion jam **130**
  Rotolo with roasted green asparagus **224**

Tomato paste
  Bean sprout omelet with sweet-and-sour ginger sauce and shiitake mushrooms **122**
  Cajun rice with bell pepper and tomato **188**
  Eggs in red wine sauce **164**
  Eggs in soy sauce **162**
  Eggs in stroganoff sauce **167**
  Flatbread with tomato **28**
  Lentil ragu with red wine and basil **144**
  Olive ragu with cherry tomatoes, polenta, and crispy basil **184**
  Polenta balls with wild garlic in smoky tomato sauce **100**
  Roasted cauliflower curry with cilantro **66**
  Sauerkraut casserole with red wine, apple, Brie, and thyme **88**
  Stifatho with eggplant and Kalamata olives **23**
  Whole-wheat lasagna with lentils and mozzarella crème **156**
Tray bake with broccoli, baby potatoes, and Vacherin Mont d'Or 74
Truffle
  Beet and quinoa burger with truffle sauce **63**
  Crispy lentil-truffle balls with truffle-Parmesan mayonnaise **107**
  Truffle risotto with mushrooms and mini burrata **123**
Truffle risotto with mushrooms and mini burrata 123

V
Vacherin Mont d'Or
  Tray bake with broccoli, baby potatoes, and Vacherin Mont d'Or **74**
Vegetarian split pea soup with dried mushrooms 158

W
Walnuts
  Baked endive with walnuts and rosemary crumb **179**
  Smoked buffalo mozzarella **138**
Warm camembert with lemon and thyme 220
Whole-wheat lasagna with lentils and mozzarella crème 156
Wild garlic
  Polenta balls with wild garlic in smoky tomato sauce **100**
Wine, red
  Eggs in red wine sauce **164**
  Giant white beans in tomato sauce with red wine, coriander seeds, and rosemary **147**
  Lentil ragu with red wine and basil **144**
  Mushroom lasagna with Parmesan béchamel sauce **126**
  Olive ragu with cherry tomatoes, polenta, and crispy basil **184**
  Sauerkraut casserole with red wine, apple, Brie, and thyme **88**
  Stifatho with eggplant and Kalamata olives **23**
  Truffle risotto with mushrooms and mini burrata **123**
Wine, white
  Arroz meloso with dry-cured olives and green asparagus **219**
  Cannellini bean purée with crème fraiche **148**
  Chickpeas with spinach in vadouvan sauce **157**
  Creamy leeks with mustard and Comté **234**
  Creamy mushroom pot pie with Riesling **129**
  Gnocchi with cavolo nero, fennel seeds, and pecorino **75**
  Kale risotto with black garlic and crispy kale **84**
  Lemon-ricotta balls with saffron cream **108**
  Mini-cannelloni with roasted sweet potatoes and buffalo mozzarella **213**
  Pasta al cartoccio with braised fennel and Stilton **229**
  Pearl couscous with fava beans and cilantro salsa verde, orange, and smoked almonds **116**
  Risotto with honey-drizzled tomatoes and buffalo ricotta **197**
  Spaghetti with purple-podded peas and cream, Parmesan, and lemon **136**
  Tray bake with broccoli, baby potatoes, and Vacherin Mont d'Or **74**

Y
Yogurt
  Cajun rice with bell pepper and tomato **188**
  Flatbread with yogurt and dill **28**
  Goat labneh with muhammara and dill **33**
  Lentil and bean tagine with cherry tomatoes and lime-infused yogurt **141**
  Marinated beets with lime, coriander seeds, and yogurt **59**
  Roasted sweet corn with garlicky yogurt and olive herb **209**

Z
Zucchini
  Harissa couscous with roasted vegetables **31**
  Roasted zucchini with chili soy sauce and sesame **37**
  Seared zucchini with Parmesan-basil hollandaise **38**
  Stuffed zucchini with herbed ricotta in puff pastry **41**
  Thai yellow curry with roasted vegetables **30**